THE COUNT OF MONTE CRISTO

by
Alexandre Dumas

Teacher Guide

Written by
Pat Watson

Note

The Tor paperback edition of the book, abridged, published by Tom Doherty Associates, LLC, ©1998, was used to prepare this guide. Page references may differ in other editions.

Please note: Please assess the appropriateness of this book for the age level and maturity of your students prior to reading and discussing it with your class.

LaLt
D891cyw

ISBN 1-58130-712-8

To order, contact your local school supply store, or—

Novel Units, Inc.
P.O. Box 791610
San Antonio, TX 78279

Web site: www.educyberstor.com

Table of Contents

Skills and Strategies

Comprehension
   Predicting, cause/effect,
   inference, time line

Writing
   Poetry, prose, dialogue,
   letter, sequel, ballad, précis

Thinking
   Research, compare/contrast,
   analysis, brainstorming,
   critical thinking

Vocabulary
   Target words, definitions,
   application

Literary Elements
   Characterization, symbolism,
   irony, personification, simile,
   metaphor, allusion, theme,
   universality, foreshadowing,
   conflict

Listening/Speaking
   Discussion, oral reading,
   poetry reading, film viewing,
   music, drama

Across the Curriculum
   Art—drawing, coat-of-arms,
   collage; History—research,
   maps

Genre: fiction

Point of View: third-person omniscient

Style: narrative

Setting: France, 1800s

Themes: vengeance, greed, love, power

Summary

A young French sailor, Edmond Dantès, is falsely accused of treason and imprisoned for fourteen years. After his miraculous escape, he finds hidden treasure and returns to France as the wealthy and prestigious Count of Monte Cristo. He implements plans for retribution on those who betrayed him, believing that he is God's instrument of vengeance. After he goes beyond the limits of rightful retaliation, he realizes that supreme power and wisdom are in God's hands alone.

Primary Characters

Edmond Dantès, the Count of Monte Cristo: protagonist; handsome, honest, humble young seaman who is wrongfully imprisoned; eventually escapes, finds hidden treasure, and returns to society as the rich, shrewd Count of Monte Cristo, intent on revenge against his enemies; other pseudonyms: English law clerk, Sinbad the Sailor, Lord Wilmore, Signor Giacomo Busoni

Louis Dantès: Edmond's father; impoverished; dies soon after Edmond's imprisonment

Abbé Faria: prisoner in Château d'If; becomes Dantès' friend and tells him about the treasure on the Isle of Monte Cristo

Monsieur Morrel: owner of the merchant ship *Pharaon*; Dantès' employer, true friend, and supporter

Maximilian and Julie Morrel; Emmanuel Herbaut: Morrel's children and son-in-law

Danglars: Dantès' jealous fellow seaman, villain who is directly responsible for Dantès' imprisonment; becomes a rich banker but loses all under vengeful hand of Count of Monte Cristo

Mme. Danglars: Danglars' wife

Eugénie Danglars: Danglars' daughter

Louise D'Armilly: Eugénie's friend and music teacher

Caderousse: neighbor of Dantès' father; knows of Danglars' plot but does not intervene; inadvertently reveals truth when Dantès returns

Mercédès: Dantès' fiancée; marries Fernand two years after Dantès' imprisonment

Fernand: Danglars' co-conspirator; marries Mercédès after Dantès' imprisonment; becomes Count de Morcerf; eventually humiliated and driven to suicide by Count's revenge

Albert de Morcerf: son of Mercédès and Fernand

Monsieur de Villefort: deputy magistrate who orders Dantès' imprisonment; becomes rich

Renee de Saint-Méran: Villefort's first wife

Valentine de Villefort: Villefort's daughter by his first wife

Marquis & Marquise de Saint-Méran: Valentine's maternal grandparents

Mme. de Villefort: Villefort's second wife; poisons victims because of money

Edward de Villefort: the Villeforts' son

Noirtier: Villefort's father; a Bonapartist

Franz d'Épinay: betrothed to Valentine

Haydee: beautiful Greek girl the Count rescues from a slave market

Luigi Vampa: bandit who kidnaps Albert de Morcerf

Major Cavalcanti and his son Andrea: imposters the Count uses to implement revenge

Bertuccio: steward to Count of Monte Cristo

Barrios: Noirtier's servant

Dr. D'Avrigny: doctor who treats poison victims

Beauchamp: newspaper editor

Lucien Debray: private secretary to Minister of Interior; involved with Mme. Danglars

Baldi: captain of the smuggler ship

Jacopo: one of crew of smuggler ship; later works for Monte Cristo

Gen. Flavien de Quesnel: royalist; grandfather of Franz d'Épinay

Background Information

Dumas based his protagonist, Edmond Dantès; i.e., the Count of Monte Cristo, on a true story he heard about a cobbler who was wrongfully imprisoned for seven years. After his release, the cobbler tracked down and killed each one of his enemies.

Historical Background

Napoleon Bonaparte (1769-1821): Italian by birth who entered the royal military school at Paris when a young boy. He was involved in the French Revolution which broke out in 1789. After varied military assignments and alliances, Napoleon eventually was named to command the French Army of Italy. In 1799, he seized power in France and in 1804, crowned himself Emperor of the French, established a new government of three members called the Consulate, and became First Consul, dictator of France. He staged war against European countries and eventually dominated much of Europe. A revolt led to Napoleon's abdication of his throne in 1814 and the crowning of Louis XVIII as king of France. Napoleon was exiled to, and became the ruler of, the tiny island of Elba off the coast of Italy. In February 1815, he sailed from Elba with 1,100 followers and began a march to Paris, where he was again hailed as emperor. This began his reign of "The Hundred Days," which ended with his defeat at Waterloo in June 1815. He was exiled to Saint Helen and died there in 1821. A follower of Napoleon was called a Bonapartist. Dumas' father was a general in Napoleon's army, and the character Noirtier in the novel is apparently patterned after Dumas' father.

Reign of Terror: the French Revolution under the Jacobin government who established a policy of terror against rebels, supporters of the king, or Girondists; 18,000 death sentences were carried out, including that of Marie Antoinette.

Marseilles: oldest and second largest city in France; country's main seaport

Monte Cristo: a small Italian island in the Mediterranean Sea, comprised primarily of a mountain of granite that rises 2,000 feet above sea level; Benedictine monks once had a monastery there.

Glossary of Titles

1. Count: nobleman equal in rank to an English earl

2. Countess: wife of a count

3. Viscount: English nobleman ranking next below an earl and above a baron; usually son of an earl

4. Comte: a count

5. Comtesse: a countess

6. Baron: nobleman of lowest hereditary rank; next below a viscount

7. Baroness: wife or widow of a baron

8. Marquis: nobleman ranking below a duke or above an earl or count

9. Marquise: wife or widow of a marquis

About the Author

Alexandre Dumas (1802-1870) was born on July 23, 1802, to Thomas-Alexandre Dumas and his wife, Marie-Louise Elisabeth. His father had served as a general under Napoleon but had fallen out of favor with him. The elder Dumas died when Alexandre was four, leaving him and his mother with limited resources. A local priest provided Dumas with limited education, and Dumas left for Paris when he was twenty-one. His first play, produced in 1829, launched his successful career as a writer and dramatist. He wrote prolifically in a wide range of genres. His most noted novels are *The Three Musketeers* (1844) and *The Count of Monte Cristo* (1844-1845). He featured continuing adventures of the Three Musketeers in *Twenty Years After* (1845) and *The Viscount of Bragelonne* (1848-1850). Dumas' well-known historical plays include *Henry III and His Court* (1829) and *The Tower of Nesle* (1832). The quality of Dumas' work and his popularity declined during France's Second Empire (1852-1870), and he was deeply in debt when he died in 1870.

Initiating Activities

Choose one or more of the following activities to establish an appropriate mindset for the novel.

1. Preview the book. Have students read the introduction and discuss the author, the setting, and the title. Elicit student response: what they have heard about and whether or not they have seen a film version.

2. Place the word "vengeance" on an overhead transparency. Brainstorm with students and cluster around the word synonyms, antonyms, causes, and results.

3. Ask students to relate prior knowledge about Napoleon Bonaparte. Present information from the Historical Background section of this guide.

4. Display a map of France and its surrounding countries. Locate Marseilles and other places as they appear in the novel.

Additional Information

Eleven movies, two TV movies, two TV series, and one mini-series have been produced to date. The most highly rated movies are the 1934 version starring Robert Donat as the Count of Monte Cristo and a television movie starring Richard Chamberlain which was produced in 1975. A new film version was released in 2002 starring James Caviezel.

Attribute Boxes

Directions: Within each box, record evidence about a character from *The Count of Monte Cristo.*

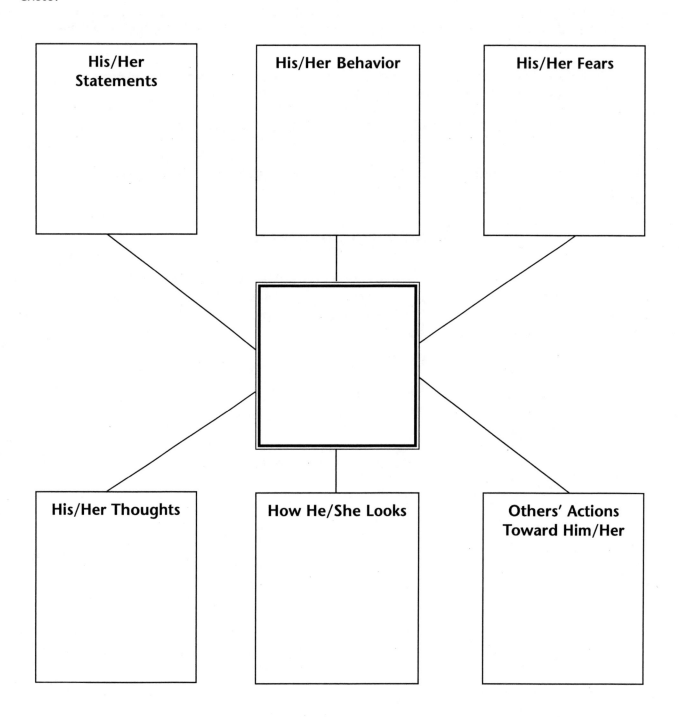

His/Her
Statements

His/Her Behavior

His/Her Fears

His/Her Thoughts

How He/She Looks

Others' Actions
Toward Him/Her

Sociogram

Directions: Complete the sociogram below by adding major and minor characters to the blank ovals. On the arrows, write a word or words to describe the relationship between the central character and the other characters. Remember, relationships go both ways, so each line requires a descriptive word. Find examples from the text to justify your answers and refer to page numbers.

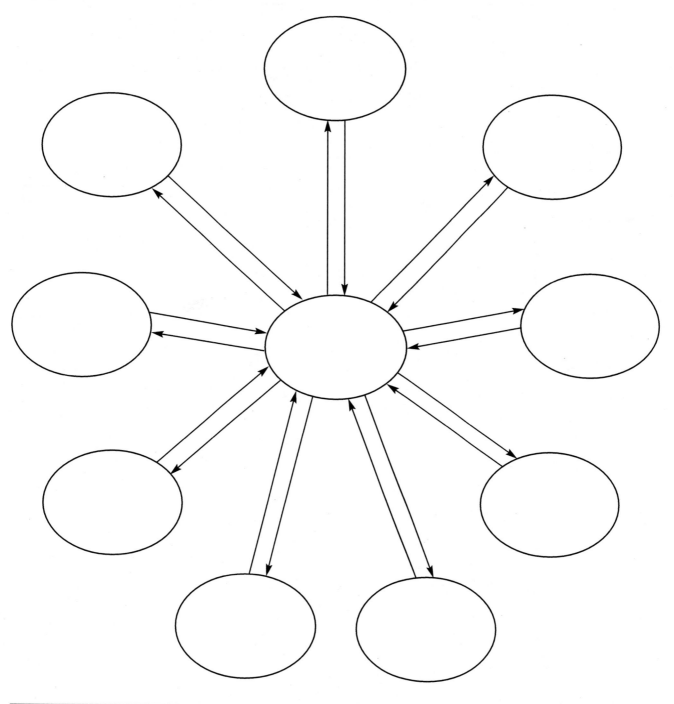

Story Map

Directions: Use the diagram below with a partner or small group to free associate thoughts about the novel after you have finished reading it. Jot down your thoughts in a similar format on a large piece of paper.

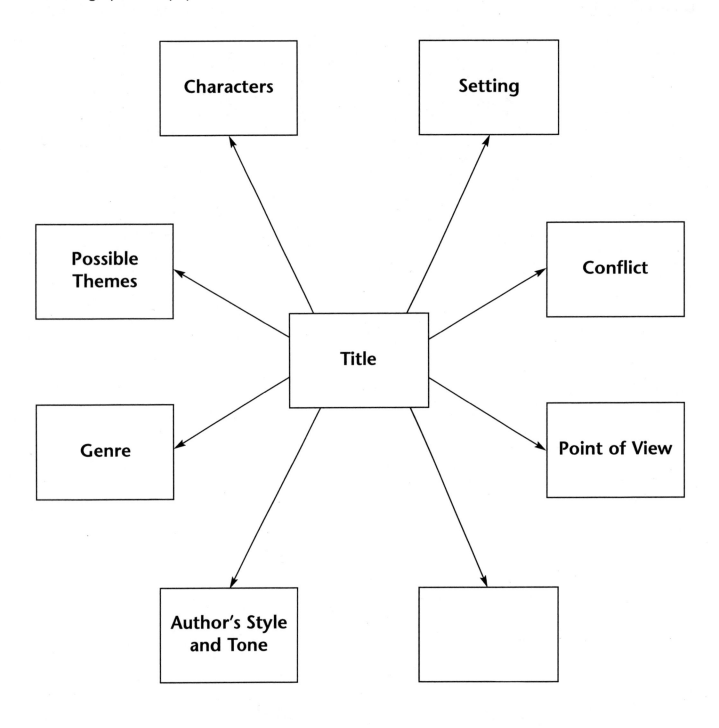

Novel Web Diagram

Directions: The oval is the place for the book's title. Fill in the boxes to summarize the story.

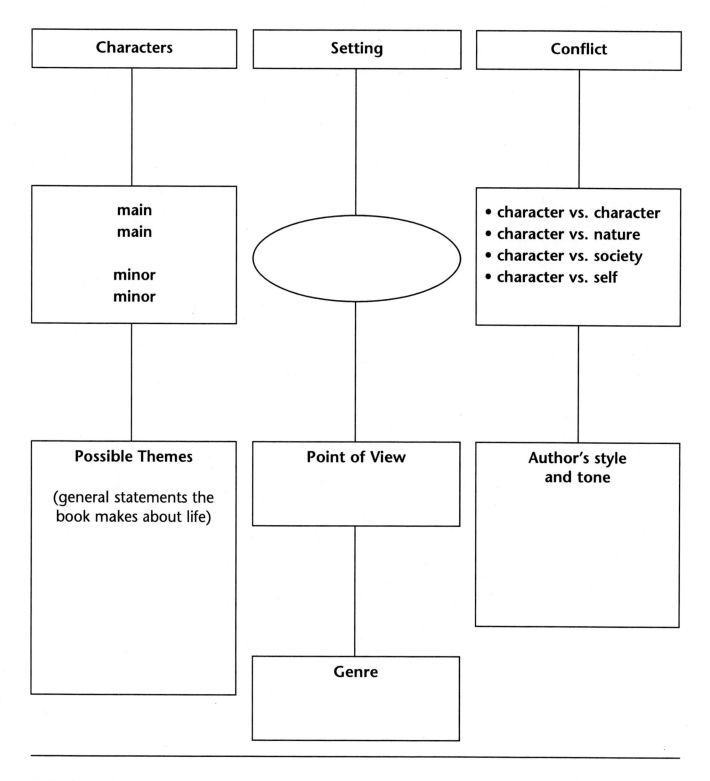

Characters	Setting	Conflict
main main minor minor		• character vs. character • character vs. nature • character vs. society • character vs. self

Possible Themes (general statements the book makes about life)	Point of View	Author's style and tone

Genre

Cause/Effect Chart

Directions: Make a flow chart to show decisions a character made, the decisions (s)he could have made, and the result(s) of each. (Use your imagination to speculate on the results of decisions the character could have made.)

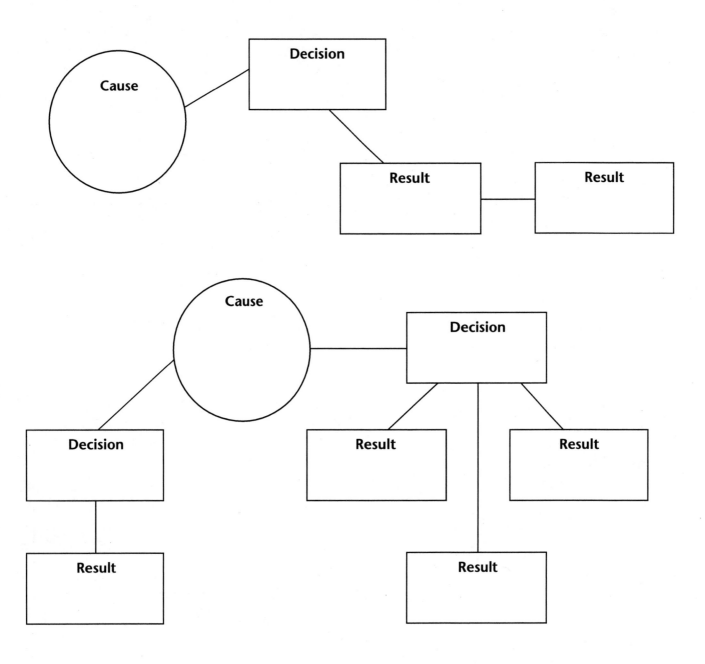

12

Chapters 1-4, pp. 1-29

Edmond Dantès, a sailor aboard the ship *Pharaon*, returns to France. He is to be named captain of the ship and plans to marry his fiancée, Mercédès. Some of his enemies conspire against him, causing him to be falsely arrested.

Vocabulary

melancholy (1)   imperceptibly (3)   obsequious (3)   vexation (15)
imperious (17)

Discussion Questions

1. Examine events aboard the *Pharaon* prior to and as it arrives in France. Discuss the importance of Dantès, Danglars, and Morrel in the opening chapter. Note the foreshadowing alluding to the Isle of Elba. *(The captain of the ship died and was buried at sea. Morrel, the owner of the ship, quizzes the young seaman Dantès. He tells Morrel about the captain's death and assures him that the cargo is safe. Danglars, the purser, is jealous of Dantès and subtly accuses him of delaying the ship by going ashore at the Isle of Elba and alludes to a letter the captain gave Dantès. Morrel plans to name Dantès as the ship's new captain. Dantès reveals existing tension between himself and Danglars. Foreshadowing: Napoleon Bonaparte, exiled self-appointed Emperor of France, retreated to and became ruler of the tiny Isle of Elba after his abdication in 1814. He returned to France in 1815 and briefly regained the monarchy but was defeated at Waterloo and was exiled to the island of St. Helene. pp. 1-9)*

2. Discuss Dantès' immediate actions after the ship lands and what this reveals. *(Dantès goes to see his father first and discovers that he has lived in poverty for many weeks because of payment of Dantès' debt to Caderousse, a tailor and neighbor. Dantès leaves his father for a joyful reunion with his fiancée, Mercédès. Prior to Dantès arrival, Mercédès' cousin Fernand proclaims his love for her and his desire to marry her. She rebuffs his proposal and vows her undying love for Dantès. pp. 9-16)*

3. Examine the interaction between Caderousse, Danglars, and Fernand. Analyze the role of each of the men in the conspiracy against Dantès. *(Dantès acts coldly toward Caderousse because of his mistreatment of Dantès' father, Danglars is jealous and bitter over Dantès' appointment as ship captain, and Dantès recognizes Fernand as an enemy because of Fernand's jealousy and bitterness over Mercédès' love for Dantès. Caderousse and Danglars meet outside Dantès' apartment and exchange words reflecting their mutual interest in Dantès' affairs. They contrive to meet Fernand after his angry departure from Mercédès and Dantès and manipulate him with flattery and arouse his jealousy. The three men form a conspiracy against Dantès. Each one is present at the betrothal feast and their actions allude to this conspiracy. Danglars' conversation with Morrel undermines Dantès' loyalty. pp. 13-14, 17-29)*

4. Analyze the implications of Dantès' arrest as a Bonapartist agent. Elicit student response to terms such as traitor, spy, conspiracy, and betrayal. *(Present information about Napoleon Bonaparte. This is found in the introductory material of this guide and at the beginning of Chapter 5. Tensions were high in 1815, following Napoleon's abdication as Emperor of France in 1814, and anyone thought to be associated with Napoleon would be suspected of conspiring*

against King Louis XVIII. If convicted of being a Bonapartist agent, Dantès will face death or imprisonment for life. pp. 25-29)

5. **Prediction:** What will happen to Dantès? to Dantès' father? to Mercédès?

Supplementary Activities

1. Display a map of France and the surrounding countries. Have students trace the path of the *Pharaon:* Smyrna, Trieste, Naples, and Marseilles (p. 1) and locate the Isle of Elba. Continue locating other places while reading the book.

2. Have students bring to class current newspaper or magazine articles involving alleged and/or convicted spies and their punishment under national law.

3. Note the following similes: Mercédès' hair...as black as jet and eyes of velvety softness of the gazelle (p. 15); Fernand recoiled like a wayfarer at the sight of a snake (p. 16); Fernand's hatred...like a powerless though furious wave (p. 17); Fernand...running like one demented (p. 17); two lovers went on their way like two of the elect on their way to Heaven (p. 21).

Chapters 5-7, pp. 29-49

Dantès is taken before Villefort on charges of treason. Villefort realizes that the Paris-bound letter Dantès received on Elba is addressed to Noirtier, Villefort's own Bonapartist father. Villefort has Dantès imprisoned in the Château d'If.

Vocabulary

usurpers (29)	royalists (30)	plebeian (31)	imprudence (39)
presentiment (44)			

Discussion Questions

1. Discuss Villefort and his father and examine their relationship. *(Villefort is deputy magistrate, 27 years old, loyal to King Louis XVIII, and engaged to a beautiful, wealthy girl. His father, Noirtier, is a Bonapartist who had been a senator under Napoleon. Villefort has distanced himself from his father and discarded the name Noirtier. Villefort must watch his own actions carefully because of the suspicions surrounding his father. pp. 29-34)*

2. Analyze Villefort's inquisition of Dantès and why he sends him to prison. *(Villefort is impressed with Dantès' answers to his questions and believes Dantès has been falsely accused because of jealousy but is loyal to the King. When he learns that the letter Dantès received on the Isle of Elba is addressed to Noirtier, Villefort realizes the precariousness of his position. Terror of losing his position and being accused of Bonapartist sympathies cause Villefort to burn the letter and send Dantès to prison. pp. 35-45)*

3. Discuss the Château d'If and its effect on Dantès. *(Only important political defendants are sent to the prison. Its name brings terror to those who are condemned to go there. Dantès tries hopelessly to hurl himself into the sea. His initial cell is a damp underground room, and he cannot eat or sleep. His repeated demands to see the governor cause him to be transferred to the dungeon where madmen are placed. pp. 45-49)*

Supplementary Activities

1. Have students research the conditions of early 19th-century French prisons.

2. Have students write a metaphor or simile poem that describes Dantès' terror. Pattern: Line 1: noun (also the title); Lines 2-4: something about the subject with each line describing the subject in a different way; Line 5: metaphor or simile that begins with the noun from line 1.

3. Analyze the similes that describe the Château d'If and Dantès' reaction to his imprisonment: a subterranean room whose bare and reeking walls seemed as though impregnated with tears (p. 46); an iron hand seemed to have nailed him to the spot where he stood the night before (p. 47); At times he would walk round and round his cell like a wild animal in a cage (p. 48).

Chapters 8-13, pp. 50-91

Mercédès and Morrel intercede in vain for Dantès. King Louis XVIII sees the rumors of Napoleon's return come true, but the coup lasts only 100 days. Villefort is promoted, Danglars departs for Spain, and Dantès' father dies. After four years in prison, Dantès and an Italian priest break through the walls that join their cells and make plans to escape.

Vocabulary

compunction (52)	benevolence (64)	despotic (77)	infamy (82)
prodigious (85)	cataleptic (88)		

Discussion Questions

1. Discuss Mercédès' visit to Villefort and analyze how one moment in time can change the course of events. *(She comes to inquire about Dantès' arrest and where he is imprisoned. Villefort is touched by her beauty and dignity and feels the weight of his own guilt. He refuses her request but, had she again begged him in the name of Almighty God, he would have relented and signed Dantès' release. Student responses to the impact of one moment in time will vary but could include last-minute pardons of those on death row, the decision to drop the first atomic bomb, etc. pp. 50-52)*

2. Discuss the political upheaval and examine Villefort's self-promotion during this time. *(King Louis XVIII has heard rumors about Napoleon's return but discounts their validity. Villefort arrives with information from the letter Dantès had been asked to deliver to Noirtier in Paris, and the King learns that Napoleon has left the Isle of Elba with three manned vessels. Villefort misrepresents Dantès' role and implies that he, Villefort, arrested Dantès and forced him to reveal the verbal message he was to deliver. A delayed telegram confirms that Napoleon has landed in France. During the King's discussion with his Minister of Police about the murder of an important general, Villefort realizes that Noirtier, his father, is the murderer. The King recognizes Villefort's loyalty and rewards him with the cross of the Legion of Honor. After Napoleon's victory, Villefort retains his position because of the influence of his father. When King Louis XVIII regains power, Villefort is promoted to Procureur du Roi. Villefort demonstrates his "loyalty" to whatever cause will benefit him most. pp. 53-63)*

15

3. Analyze Dantès' reaction to his imprisonment and his "journey" from despair to hope. Elicit student response to the value of "little things" and the importance of human contact. *(At first he unsuccessfully prays to his jailers. When that fails, he turns to God but begins to scream blasphemies when he remains a prisoner. He begins to plot vengeance against the men who were instrumental in his imprisonment. He longs for death and decides to starve himself. As death approaches, Dantès hears a sound that indicates another human is digging to get to his cell. Despair turns to hope. He becomes grateful to God for simple things such as the iron handle of a saucepan. Dantès begins to dig toward the other prisoner and to cry out for God's help. pp. 65-69)*

4. Discuss the abbé and his effect on Dantès. *(Abbé Faria, an Italian scholar who appears to be in his middle sixties, has been a political prisoner since 1807 and has been in Château d'If since 1811. He is ingenious, having made paper and quills and having devised methods to write volumes of his thoughts. It took him four years to make tools, and he has been digging for two years, thinking he was digging toward the outside wall of the prison. Although he is disappointed when he realizes he has been digging toward Dantès' cell, they delight in each other's company. Dantès has renewed hope and faith. They begin planning to escape together. The abbé guides Dantès as he explores who is responsible for his imprisonment and why: Danglars, who was jealous and wrote the anonymous letter to Villefort; Fernand, who wanted Mercédès; Villefort, whom the abbé recognizes as the son of Noirtier. Dantès vows vengeance on them all. pp. 72-84)*

5. **Prediction:** Will Dantès escape the Château d'If?

Supplementary Activities

1. Have students research and report to the class on either the Reign of Terror or the Hundred Days.

2. Note the literary devices: **Metaphor**—Isle of Elba: volcano (p. 55); gaoler: living door, bar of flesh (p. 72) **Similes**—Mercédès would stand as motionless as a statue (p. 64); ship...shiver and shake like a feather in the hand of a giant (p. 66); the abbé lights Dantès' mind like the aurora borealis lights the navigator's path (p. 85); the abbé lay as inert as a block of wood, whiter and colder than marble, more crushed than a reed trampled underfoot (p. 89) **Personification**—Death smiles on me (p. 66).

Chapters 14-17, pp. 91-122

Realizing he is physically unable to escape, the abbé reveals to Dantès a tale of hidden treasure on the Isle of Monte Cristo. The abbé dies, and Dantès escapes from Château d'If by masquerading as the corpse.

Vocabulary

requiem (107)   torpid (113)   misanthropy (119)   chimerical (120)

Discussion Questions

1. Discuss the abbé's disclosure of the secret to the treasure he believes is buried on the Isle of Monte Cristo. *(The abbé has a cataleptic fit when he and Dantès are preparing to escape. Dantès vows he will never leave the abbé alone but will help him escape from prison. The abbé shows Dantès a portion of a will from the murdered Caesar Spada, left in a breviary he bequeathed to the abbé. One-third of it had been destroyed by fire, but the abbé has been able to supply the missing words and discover directions to hidden treasure on the Isle of Monte Cristo. The abbé was arrested and imprisoned before he could search for the treasure. He calls Dantès the "child of his captivity," and has Dantès memorize the instructions and tells him they will each have half of the treasure or, if the abbé dies, it will all belong to Dantès. pp. 91-102)*

2. Examine Dantès' escape, including the "coincidences," and elicit student response for the plausibility of such an escape. *(The abbé has a third attack and dies, despite Dantès' valiant efforts to save him. The jailers place the body in a cloth bag. Dantès re-enters the abbé's cell, removes the body and takes it to his own cell, then gets into the bag and sews it back together. He plans to cut his way out after he is placed in the grave. The bag is thrown into the sea with a cannonball weight, and Dantès barely escapes his watery grave; Coincidences: the abbé is buried at night when Dantès' trickery will be least detectable; Dantès cuts the cord around his feet just in time; he sees five fishermen clinging to a boat that crashes against the rocks, killing all five, and he retrieves the cap of one of the dead sailors for a disguise. The crew of the smuggler ship that saves him accepts Dantès' explanation of the firing of the cannon at Château d'If; the skipper of the ship chooses the Isle of Monte Cristo to unload his cargo. pp. 108-122)*

3. Analyze the implications of Dantès' "baptism." Note the contrast between a "baptism to life" and Dantès' "baptism to death." *(When the prison guards throw Dantès into the sea and he emerges alive, he is transformed into the Count of Monte Cristo. He has languished in prison for fourteen years, becoming bitter and suspicious as he plots vengeance against his enemies. He has lost his youth, his innocence, and his plans for the future. He is now deceitful and filled with the desire for revenge. Lying comes easily to him during his first interaction with humans, and this sets the stage for his future. Instead of a rebirth to a new, better life, as is usually symbolized by baptism, Dantès' is a baptism of death: the death of his conscience, his integrity, and his compassion. Inference)*

4. **Prediction:** Will Dantès find the treasure? If so, how will it change his life?

Supplementary Activities

1. Have students write a short poem that reflects Dantès' feeling of being totally alone after the abbé dies.

2. Read aloud the directions to the hidden treasure (p. 101). Have a student draw a treasure map.

3. Note the similes: [Dantès] passed through the air like a wounded bird falling...dropped like an arrow (p. 111); granite giant rose like menacing phantom...dark summit appeared like an arm stretched out to seize its prey (p. 112); rocks looking like an immense fire (p. 113); [Dantès] clung to his rock like a limpet (p. 113).

Chapters 18-22, pp. 122-150

Dantès finds the hidden treasure on the Isle of Monte Cristo. He returns to France disguised as a priest and learns what has happened to the primary characters in his former life.

Vocabulary

rendezvous (122)   labyrinth (124)   intrepid (128)   ironical (138)
conscription (145)

Discussion Questions

1. Discuss Dantès' discovery of the treasure on the Isle of Monte Cristo and analyze the ongoing changes in him since his escape from prison. *(He pretends to be seriously injured and insists that the crew of the Jeune Amélie leave him on the island. He discovers the location of Spada's cave and uses gunpowder to blast away the surface rock. He discovers untold wealth in a wooden chest; Changes: he had previously wanted only liberty, but now he desires riches. He has become deceptive; e.g., wants no one around him, lies about being injured, and lies about his sudden wealth. pp. 122-133)*

2. Describe Dantès' return to France and examine what he learns about the principal characters in his life prior to his imprisonment. Identify his pseudonym and examine its effectiveness. *(A shipmate first goes to Marseilles and reports to Dantès the news of his father's death and Mercédès' disappearance. Dantès returns to France, disguised as a priest in whom Dantès had confided before his death, asking him to "remove the tarnish from his name." Dantès encounters Caderousse, entices him with a diamond, and manipulates him into relating the events leading to and following Dantès' imprisonment. Dantès' father: died of grief and hunger; Morrel: attempted to clear Dantès' name and took care of his father; Fernand and Danglars: betrayed Dantès, Fernand for love of Mercédès and Danglars because of jealous ambition; Danglars wrote the defamatory letter and Fernand mailed it; Caderousse kept silent; Mercédès: married Fernand and has a son, Albert. Morrel faces bankruptcy; Danglars and Fernand, now the Count of Morcerf, are wealthy; Caderousse lives in poverty. pp. 135-150)*

Supplementary Activities

1. Prepare a chart for an overhead transparency on which you list Dantès and each of his pseudonyms in a box on the left-hand side. In a box opposite each alias, place the names of the characters with whom he interacts as that character. This is an ongoing activity to be completed as the novel is read.

2. Have students write a name poem for each of Dantès' pseudonyms. Pattern: place the letters of the name vertically on the paper; for each letter, write a word or phrase that describes the character or tells something about him.

3. Have students write a name poem for Caderousse.

4. Note the literary devices: **Similes**—Dantès, jumping like a chamois (p. 124); lizards bright as emeralds (p. 126); facets of granite sparkled like diamonds (p. 129); Dantès could not waste his time looking at his gold and diamonds like a dragon guarding a useless treasure (p. 132) **Metaphors**—stars: God's lanterns (p. 122) **Allusions**—"Now, open, Sesame!" (p. 126): taken

---

from the story of "Ali Baba and the Forty Thieves" from the *Arabian Nights*; Hercules (p. 127): one of greatest heroes of Greek mythology; Titans (p. 128): first gods in Greek mythology; Pont du Gard (p. 135): famous Roman aqueduct across the river near Nimes, France
Personification—Dame Fortune (p. 149)

Chapters 23-25, pp. 150-174

Dantès, disguised as a law firm clerk, learns what the prison records say about Dantès' imprisonment and finds that he is presumed dead. He rescues Morrel from financial ruin.

Vocabulary

inveterate (155)   probity (159)   verity (164)   repugnance (167)

Discussion Questions

1. Analyze why Dantès assumes the identity of a law clerk for the firm of Thomson and French of Rome. *(In this capacity, he has access to the prison records and discovers that Dantès was arrested on charges of being a Bonapartist agent, that Morrel interceded for him, and that Dantès is presumed dead following an unsuccessful escape attempt. Villefort signed the charges against Dantès and the orders for his imprisonment. This disguise also enables Dantès to save Morrel from bankruptcy in the name of the law firm he allegedly represents. pp. 150-166)*

2. Characterize Morrel. Discuss the changes in his fortunes and his attempts to recover. Elicit student response to Morrel's "final" solution (pp. 165, 170-172) and contrast the "honor" of 19th-century France and the alternatives a man of honor has today. *(He is honest and fulfills his obligations promptly even when he must sell personal belongings to do so. He appeals to Danglars, who refuses to help him. His shipyard is almost deserted, and only two employees remain. Filled with anxiety, he pins his last hopes on return of the* Pharaon. *When he discovers the ship is lost, he submits to "God's will" and pays the crew with his last money. Dantès [as the law clerk] gives him a reprieve. Morrel later plans to commit suicide rather than fail to keep his word. pp. 155-172)*

3. Note the emergence of Maximilian and Julie Morrel. Examine their relationship with their father. Tell students the Morrel children will be important later in the development of the plot. *(Maximilian, the son, and Julie, the daughter, love and respect their father and are willing to do anything they can to save the company. Maximilian accepts his father's suicide solution and vows to redeem the family name. It is through Julie that Sinbad the Sailor assists Morrel. pp. 156-174)*

4. Analyze Dantès' (as Sinbad) parting words, "Now, farewell to kindness, humanity, gratitude..." *(He has fulfilled a vow to repay Morrel's goodness and will no longer play the part of Providence in recompensing the good but will act as the god of vengeance to punish the wicked. He will avenge himself against Villefort, Danglars, Fernand, and Mercédès. p. 174)*

5. **Prediction:** How will Dantès implement his plan for revenge?

Supplementary Activities

1. Add the law clerk and Sinbad the Sailor to Dantès' aliases. Note their interactions with the Morrel family.

2. Have students list characteristics of a "man of honor."

3. Have students analyze the irony of the disguised Dantès listening to the tale of himself as told by M. de Boville (pp. 153-154).

Chapters 26-29, pp. 174-217

Dantès emerges in Rome as the Count of Monte Cristo. He rescues Albert Morcerf—Mercédès and Fernand's son—from bandits and asks Albert to introduce him to Paris society in three months.

Vocabulary

cicerone (175)   dissertations (184)   alacrity (206)   catacombs (208)

Discussion Questions

1. Characterize the Count of Monte Cristo and discuss his interactions with Albert de Morcerf and Franz d'Épinay. *(He is immensely rich, handsome, supposedly Sicilian or Maltese, generous, gentlemanly, has informants in the pope's palace in Rome, and is powerful. He offers them his friendship and gives them access to his transportation and accommodations. pp. 174, 182-194)*

2. Examine the importance of Luigi Vampa. *(He is a bandit, has committed murder, kidnaps foreigners and kills them if ransom is not paid. He kidnaps Albert but releases him to Monte Cristo in exchange for the delay of Peppino's execution. Monte Cristo asks Albert, whom he now knows is the son of Fernand and Mercédès, to introduce him in Paris. pp. 178-179, 202-217)*

3. Examine the statement, "It was as though Rome had been changed by the magic breath of some demon of darkness into a vast tomb." *(This foreshadows Albert's kidnapping and imprisonment in the catacombs of Rome. Luigi Vampa: the "demon of darkness"; the catacombs: the tomb. p. 202)*

4. **Prediction:** Note Franz's premonition about the Count. How will this premonition come true?

Supplementary Activities

1. Have students bring to class pictures of Rome. Compare with places mentioned in this section; e.g., St. Peter's, the Colosseum, and the catacombs.

2. Have students research public executions of 19th-century Italy.

3. Note the allusions: St. Peter's (p. 177): first important Christian basilica; Pope Gregory XVI (p. 197): conservative Pope of 1800s; Stoics (p. 193): philosophers who emphasize the role of fate in men's lives; catacombs of Saint Sebastian (p. 208): located on outskirts of Rome, one of the most famous

4. Analyze the simile, "His [Dantès'] hand was as cold as a corpse" (p. 217). Note the importance of Dantès' "return from the dead" as the Count of Monte Cristo.

Chapters 30-33, pp. 218-256

The Count of Monte Cristo is introduced to Parisian society and "meets" Fernand, Mercédès, and Danglars. He attains a large amount of credit at Danglars' bank. Note the convergence of the primary characters throughout this section.

Vocabulary

philanthropic (223)	cosmopolitan (226)	prosaic (230)	antipathy (235)
importunate (239)	perspicacious (240)	filial (242)	

Discussion Questions

1. Analyze Monte Cristo's visit to Albert's home in Paris. Contrast Dantès' life for the past several years with the status of the Morcerfs. *(Albert's parents, Mercédès and Fernand, are making preparations to honor Monte Cristo. The Morcerfs have attained wealth, a beautiful home, and societal influence. By contrast, Dantès, although now wealthy, spent many of the past years in a prison dungeon, with meager food and only one friend. This section reintroduces Maximilian Morrel as a friend of Albert, and Albert alludes to Danglars and his family. Monte Cristo learns from Maximilian that Julie and Emmanuel are married. He observes a portrait of Mercédès as he remembers her and is introduced to Fernand and Mercédès. Monte Cristo observes secret grief in Fernand's careworn features. Mercédès experiences a strange terror, probes Albert about Monte Cristo, and cautions him to be careful. pp. 218-242)*

2. Discuss Monte Cristo's visit to and business dealings with Danglars. Analyze the significance of his purchase of Danglars' horses. *(Monte Cristo's ability to manipulate the Danglars is obvious throughout this section. Danglars is reluctant to issue "unlimited" credit for Monte Cristo, but agrees to do so when the Count alludes to other firms who will be glad to honor his request. They settle on the sum of six million for the first year, an amount that astonishes Danglars. Monte Cristo purchases Danglars' grappled grey horses, which actually belong to Madame Danglars, for a phenomenal sum, causing her to become violently angry. Thus, he achieves his objective: destroying the peace in the family and enabling him to win the Danglars' gratitude by returning the horses. Mme. Danglars loans the horses to Mm. de Villefort, and Monte Cristo devises a way to have the horses run away and be stopped in front of his house, endearing himself to Mme. de Villefort. pp. 242-256)*

3. Note the foreshadowing of Monte Cristo's statement to Danglars, "You will know more about it (the family treasure), though, in a short time" (p. 248). **Prediction:** When, why, and how will Danglars learn about the Count's fortune?

Supplementary Activities

1. Have interested students draw a caricature of Danglars based on the metaphors with which Monte Cristo portrays him: snake, vulture, buzzard (p. 243).

2. Have students write a cinquain poem, "Dame Fortune," based on Monte Cristo's personification of Fortune. (p. 237). Pattern: Line 1: title; Line 2: two words to describe the title; Line 3: three words to express action concerning the title; Line 4: four words to express feelings about the title; Line 5: a synonym for the title.

Chapters 34-37, pp. 257-283

Monte Cristo visits with Haydee, the young Greek girl he rescued from the slave market. He goes to the home of M. Morrel's children. He and Mme. de Villefort discuss poison. He plans to invite the Danglars and the Villeforts for dinner at his home.

Vocabulary

sonorous (258)   pseudonym (265)   toxicology (267)   taciturn (268)
candid (280)

Discussion Questions

1. Discuss Haydee. Elicit student response concerning her role in Monte Cristo's life. *(She is a beautiful Greek girl whom the Count rescued from the slave market. He assures her she is free, but she considers herself to be his slave. She is content to live secluded and expresses deep love for him. He cautions her not to reveal the secret of her birth. pp. 257-261)*

2. Discuss the importance of Monte Cristo's visit to the Morrel family. Note the irony of Julie's statement, "He (God) did for us what He only does for His elect: He sent us one of His angels" (p. 263). *(Julie is happily married to Emmanuel, her father's former clerk, where Monte Cristo sees the purse from "Sinbad the Sailor." Julie and Maximilian reveal the deeds of and their gratefulness toward their "angel," whom their father believed to be Edmond Dantès. Irony: They are talking to the angel. pp. 261-266)*

3. Analyze the importance of Monte Cristo's visit to the Villeforts. Note Mme. de Villefort's consuming love for her son, Edward. Analyze the metaphorical content of the Count's statement, "I am convinced that the seed I have sown has not fallen on barren ground" (p. 276). *(Monte Cristo meets Villefort's children: Valentine, who is betrothed to Albert, and Edward. He learns that Noirtier, Villefort's father, lives with them but is completely paralyzed. He recalls to Mme. de Villefort a prior meeting when they discussed the poison brucine, and he gives her some of the poison. Metaphor: seed: use of poison; ground: Mme. de Villefort's mind. This chapter foreshadows Mme. de Villefort's poisoning of several people, including her own son. pp. 267-276)*

4. Examine Monte Cristo's proposed invitation to the Danglars and the Villeforts to his home but the exclusion of the Morcerfs. *(He plans to further his revenge by introducing them to the Cavalcantis, who will manipulate the two families financially and personally, and does not wish to involve or hurt Mercédès. He alludes to his desire to attain Mercédès' esteem. pp. 280-283)*

5. **Prediction:** What will happen in the betrothals of Valentine de Villefort to Franz d'Épinay and Eugénie Danglars to Albert de Morcerf?

Supplementary Activity

Analyze the significance of the allusions: King Mithridates (p. 271): ancient ruler who fought three wars against Rome and allegedly ingested poison gradually in order to build an immunity against it; Lady Macbeth (p. 274): encouraged Macbeth to murder King Duncan and seize his throne, primarily because of her maternal instincts. *(The Count alludes to both of these to instill in Mme. de Villefort's mind how and why she must use the poison.)*

Chapters 38-42, pp. 284-320

Valentine secretly meets Maximilian Morrel, whom she loves. Noirtier, Valentine's grandfather, loves her and tries to protect her from marriage to Franz by excluding her from his will. Monte Cristo implements his plans for the destruction of Danglars' finances.

Vocabulary

avaricious (287)	notary (297)	approbation (298)	propriety (303)
patriarch (306)	pecuniary (307)	nabob (319)	conjugal (320)

Discussion Questions

1. Examine the interweaving of characters from Dantès' past and the Count's influence in their lives. *(Valentine de Villefort loves Maximilian Morrel; Eugénie Danglars is betrothed to Albert de Morcerf but does not love him; Noirtier, Villefort's father, lives in the Villefort home. Maximilian tells the Count about his love for Valentine. pp. 284-291)*

2. Discuss the Villeforts' and Noirtier's opinions toward the impending marriage of Valentine and Franz d'Épinay. Note the reference to Quesnel, Franz's father; refer back to Quesnel's disappearance, pp. 60-61. *(Noirtier and Franz's father were political enemies, and Noirtier opposes the marriage. Villefort feels it is a good move politically and will allay suspicions about Villefort's suspected involvement in the assassination of Franz's father. Mme. de Villefort secretly hopes the marriage will not occur. pp. 292-296, 303, 307)*

3. Analyze Noirtier's solution to the marriage and the reactions of those involved. *(He has the notary prepare a will that excludes Valentine, believing Franz will not want to marry her if she has no inheritance. Valentine is grateful, Villefort is angry but insists the marriage will take place anyway, Mme. de Villefort is pleased. pp. 297-304)*

4. Analyze how Monte Cristo implements his plans for revenge. Elicit student response to the Cavalcantis and the role they will play in the Count's plans. *(He sends a telegram, reprinted in the newspaper, that causes Danglars to lose a million francs; he arranges a meeting between Danglars and the imposters Cavalcanti and his son. Chapter 65 reveals how this leads to Danglars' further financial ruin and Eugénie Danglars' disgrace because of Andrea de Calvalcanti. pp. 309, 314-320)*

Supplementary Activities

1. Have students stage the conversation between the notary and Noirtier.

2. Analyze Noirtier's condition as described in the literary devices: **Similes**—[Noirtier's mind] flickering like a lamp waiting to be extinguished (pp. 270-271); [Noirtier's] sight and hearing like two sparks that animate his body (pp. 291-292) **Metaphor**—Noirtier: lump of clay (p. 292)

3. Note the literary devices: **Similes**—telegraph lines shining in sun like spiders' legs (p. 308); [The Count's house] awakened from its long sleep like Sleeping Beauty's castle in the wood (p. 311) **Allusion**—Nero (p. 317): Roman Emperor A.D. 54-68

Chapters 43-46, pp. 320-353

Danglars blames his wife and Debray, with whom she is having an affair, for further financial losses. Monte Cristo plants the thought in Danglars' mind of a marriage between Eugénie and Andrea de Cavalcanti. Mercédès' veiled comments in a conversation with the Count reveal that she recognizes him. Valentine's maternal grandfather, Saint-Méran, dies suddenly.

Vocabulary

presages (327)	sardonic (330)	condescension (334)	eccentric (338)
banalities (340)	decorum (349)	apoplectic (352)	

Discussion Questions

1. Analyze Danglars' accusations toward his wife and their significance. *(Although he acknowledges that she has given him tips that enabled him to make money, he points out that each time she enriched herself. He now blames her for financial losses incurred when she gave him false information and accuses her of giving money to Debray. He implies that his wife and Debray are romantically involved and demands that Debray return the money she has given him. Significance: He blames his wife but does not suspect the Count. pp. 320-326)*

2. Examine Monte Cristo's manipulation of Danglars regarding the Morcerfs. *(By introducing Danglars to the Cavalcantis and implying what a perfect husband Andrea would make, Monte Cristo causes Danglars to reconsider Eugénie's marriage to Albert. Danglars views the Cavalcantis as people of "old money," and reveals to Monte Cristo that he knew Morcerf when he was the poor fisherman Fernand. Monte Cristo places in Danglars' mind the idea of finding out what role Fernand played in the Ali Pasha affair. In Chapter 50, Haydee reveals that the Ali Pasha was her father. pp. 328-332)*

3. Analyze Monte Cristo's visit to the Morcerfs' home. *(He goes to a ball there but refuses to accept any sort of food. He and Mercédès converse. Through veiled questions, she shows that she recognizes him. He reveals that he has suffered deeply, and tells her about his lost love. He tells her that Haydee is a slave whom he has adopted as a daughter. pp. 340-347)*

4. Discuss the implications of the death of Saint-Méran. *(The Saint-Mérans are Valentine's maternal grandparents and were coming to hasten her marriage to Franz. Her grandmother feels she, too, will die soon, and fears she has been poisoned by an apparition that appeared in the night. Her symptoms arouse the doctor's suspicions. Refer to this section when students read Chapters 47, 60-63. pp. 346-353)*

5. **Prediction:** What has happened to the Saint-Mérans?

Supplementary Activities

1. Have students write a five-senses poem about Greed. Pattern: Line 1: color of the emotion; Line 2: sound of the emotion; Line 3: taste of the emotion; Line 4: smell of the emotion; Line 5: sight (what the emotion looks like); Line 6: feeling evoked by the emotion.

2. Have two students read aloud the conversation between the Count and Mercédès (pp. 344-346).

3. Analyze the simile, "A careworn capitalist is like a comet" (p. 327).

Chapters 47-49, pp. 353-394

Maximilian and Valentine decide to elope. Madame Saint-Méran dies from poison. Noirtier reveals that he killed Franz's father. Danglars' financial reverses continue.

Vocabulary

dispassionately (356)	ineffable (359)	austere (368)	adherent (379)
reparation (383)	dexterity (389)		

Discussion Questions

1. Examine the conversation between Maximilian and Valentine. Note Maximilian's melodramatic pleas. *(She tells him she must marry Franz in honor of her grandmother's wishes. Maximilian wants her to elope with him, but she at first refuses. He implores her with the scenario of being totally alone if she marries Franz and threatens to commit suicide if she does so. She finally agrees to elope. pp. 353-358)*

2. Analyze the conversation Maximilian overhears between Villefort and Doctor d'Avrigny. What does this lead Maximilian to do? *(He is waiting for Valentine, who fails to appear for their rendezvous. Villefort and the doctor appear in the garden and discuss the terrible death of Valentine's grandmother, Madame de Saint-Méran. The doctor tells Villefort that he is convinced she died from the poison brucine. Note the conversation between Mme. de Villefort and the Count about brucine, pp. 272-273. Maximilian scales the wall and enters the house to find Valentine. pp. 361-366)*

3. Examine the role Valentine's grandfather, Noirtier, plays in her life and discuss her and Maximilian's visit to him. *(She loves her grandfather deeply and feels he is the only friend she has in the world. She feels that she and Maximilian need him, takes Maximilian to meet him, and pleads with him to help her marry Maximilian. Although Noirtier is paralyzed, he communicates well with Valentine, and he tells them to wait and that he will save her from marrying Franz. pp. 366-379)*

4. Examine how Noirtier saves Valentine from marrying Franz. *(He asks to speak with Franz, whose full name is Franz de Quesnel. He directs his servant to retrieve a document from a secret drawer that reveals that he, Noirtier, is the Bonapartist who killed Franz's father, General de Quesnel. Refer to the description of the man suspected of killing Quesnel, p. 61. Franz will never consent to marry the granddaughter of his father's killer. pp. 371-387, 390)*

5. Analyze Monte Cristo's continuing manipulation of Danglars. *(He causes him to continue to lose money; influences push toward marriage between Eugénie and Andrea de Cavalcanti, Danglars has discovered Fernand's role in Janina. pp. 388-389)*

6. **Prediction:** What has Danglars discovered about Fernand and Janina and how will this affect the story line?

Supplementary Activities

1. Have students research the poison brucine (strychnine, p. 364): type, derivative, legal uses, symptoms of ingestion, treatment. Students should report their findings and compare with details in novel.

2. Ask interested students to stage Noirtier's interaction with Valentine and Morrel or with Franz.

3. Note the allusion to Goethe's heroes (p. 388). Goethe: German poet, novelist, and playwright; masterpiece, "Faust."

Chapters 50-53, pp. 394-434

Haydee relates to Albert the story of her father, Ali Tebelin, and of the trusted French officer's (Fernand's) treachery in his death. Danglars nullifies the engagement between his daughter and Albert, and he releases to the newspaper the story of Fernand's betrayal in Janina. Noirtier's servant, Barrios, dies from poison, and the doctor implicates Valentine in the deaths of her grandparents and Barrios.

Vocabulary

contemptuous (399)	injunction (401)	firman (409)	hashish (412)
cryptic (417)	calumnies (418)	incessant (430)	phenomena (431)
flagrant (432)			

Discussion Questions

1. Summarize Haydee's story and analyze the implications for Monte Cristo's plans for revenge. Note Albert's response to her father's name and discuss why the Count cautions him that he must not reveal his father's service under the Ali Pasha. *(When Haydee was four years old, her father, Ali Tebelin, Pasha of Janina, and his family flee from an insurrection and impending seizure by the Sultan's delegate. Ali Tebelin sends a trusted French officer [actually Fernand] to the Sultan to seek a pardon. He has arranged with a trusted servant to destroy everything if the answer is negative. The French officer deceives him into thinking the pardon has come, Ali Tebelin and his men die, and Haydee and her mother are taken as slaves by their new master [Fernand]. He, in turn, sells them to slave merchants. Haydee's mother dies and a rich American buys Haydee, who then sells her to a Sultan. The Count of Monte Cristo buys her from the Sultan. Before hearing Haydee's story, Albert tells Monte Cristo that his father had served under Ali Tebelin. Monte Cristo cautions him not to reveal his father's name because he is afraid Haydee will recognize the name of her father's betrayer. pp. 394-412)*

2. Discuss the conversation between Danglars and Morcerf (Fernand) and the ensuing events. Elicit student responses concerning Monte Cristo's involvement. *(Morcerf comes to Danglars to ask for Eugénie's hand in marriage for Albert and reminds him of their agreement eight years ago. Danglars tells Morcerf the contract is null and void, tells him that neither Mercédès nor the Morcerfs' fortune is responsible, and alludes to slander against Morcerf himself. An article in the newspaper the next morning reveals the story of Fernand's treachery in the Ali Tebelin debacle. Danglars is pleased with the written report and knows explanations for the broken engagement will not be needed. pp. 415-419)*

3. Analyze circumstances surrounding Barrios' death, the implications, and the ramifications for Valentine. *(He dies after drinking lemonade which had been prepared for Noirtier and offered to him by Valentine. The doctor finds poison in the lemonade, but Noirtier would not have been affected because he has been receiving small doses daily as treatment for his paralysis. The doctor believes the murderer did not know of Noirtier's immunity and that Barrios died in the place of his master. The doctor accuses Valentine of the series of poisonings because she is the one who would benefit from the deaths of her grandparents. Villefort refuses to "drag his daughter into the hands of the executioners," and the doctor warns him about further incidents. pp. 422-434)*

4. **Prediction:** What will happen to Valentine? Will there be other deaths? If so, who will die?

Supplementary Activities

1. Analyze the following allusions and their significance to the story line: Catherine de' Medici (p. 394): She was a powerful woman during the reign of her son, King Charles IX. During the St. Bartholomew Day massacre, Catholics killed thousands of Huguenots. Catherine is traditionally blamed for ordering the massacre; Shakespeare's Polonius (p. 431): the king's advisor who is eavesdropping for the king when Hamlet stabs and kills him.

2. Have students write a metaphor poem for Betrayal.

3. Note the similes: [Haydee's father] drove us [her and her mother] before him as a shepherd drives his straggling flock (p. 402); our bark sped like the wind (p. 402); [Haydee's] head fell into her hands like a flower bowed down by the force of the storm (p. 406); one single light shone...like a solitary star (p. 406); flames rushed up as from the crater of a volcano (p. 410); disappeared in a blaze of fire...as though hell had opened under his feet (p. 410); [Morrel] as pale as if he had seen a snake start up to attack him (p. 423); [Barrios] fell back as though struck by lightning (p. 428); [the doctor's] respect for Villefort and friendship for his family like two bandages before his eyes (p. 430); Valentine...pure as a lily and whose heart is of gold (p. 432); Action [of poison] as quick as thought, rapid as lightning, deadly as a thunderbolt (p. 433); shame and remorse eat into conscience like a worm (p. 434); smile...like a meteor passing ominously between two clouds (p. 434)

Chapters 54-59, pp. 434-475

Fernand is found guilty of felony, treason, and dishonor. Albert challenges Monte Cristo to a duel when he discovers his involvement in his father's ruin. Mercédès comes to Monte Cristo and begs for her son's life. He reveals to her the truth about his imprisonment. Albert apologizes to Monte Cristo, saving both of their lives. Fernand discovers Monte Cristo's true identity, loses everything, and kills himself.

Vocabulary

defamatory (435)	compatriots (438)	cognizant (446)	odious (459)
apparition (474)			

Discussion Questions

1. Examine the circumstances surrounding Morcerf's (Fernand's) trial. *(He appears at the Chamber of Peers, unaware of the defamatory article about his treachery in Janina. The article is read aloud and the time is set for his inquiry. Fernand defends himself by showing them the Ali Tebelin's ring and letters of trust. He tells them that, when he returned to defend the Pasha, he was dead. He says that the Pasha left his wife and daughter in his [Fernand's] care but they had disappeared when he returned and that no one is left to corroborate his story. The President of the Chamber of Peers reads a letter from someone proclaiming to be an eyewitness to the slaughter of Ali Tebelin. Haydee then appears and relates her story and presents her bill of sale from the Sultan to the Count of Monte Cristo. Haydee vows that the Count knows nothing of her appearance and is out of the country. She identifies Fernand as her father's betrayer. He is found guilty of felony, treason, and dishonor by a unanimous vote. pp. 434-445)*

2. Discuss why Albert challenges the Count of Monte Cristo to a duel and the ensuing events. *(Albert confronts Danglars about the letter of inquiry to Janina. Danglars implicates the Count of Monte Cristo. Albert believes Monte Cristo is responsible for his father's ruin and challenges him to a duel. Monte Cristo accepts the challenge and the duel is arranged. Mercédès pleads for her son's life. Monte Cristo tells her why he must avenge himself against Fernand but finally agrees to allow Albert to live, believing he himself must die instead. Mercédès tells Albert the truth about his father, he apologizes to Monte Cristo, and they both live. pp. 445-466)*

3. Analyze Monte Cristo's allusions to God's providence in appointing him to the role of avenger. Elicit student response as to whether or not he has a right to vengeance and if they view him as God's instrument. *(He alludes to the true cause of the duel, known only to God and himself, and his assurance that God will be on his side. He tells Mercédès that Fernand is not suffering a misfortune but a punishment inflicted by the work of Providence. Monte Cristo views himself as betrayed, assassinated, and cast into a tomb, but raised from that tomb by God's grace for the purpose of fulfilling God's purpose by punishing Fernand. pp. 455-459)*

4. Examine the conversation between Monte Cristo (Edmond) and Mercédès. Analyze the metaphors for Edmond: "The lion was tamed, the avenger was overcome!" and "Death will return to its tomb, the phantom to darkness!" (p. 461) *(She tells him she recognized him when she first saw him. She detects Edmond's venomous hatred toward Fernand and tries to explain why Albert is so angry. Mercédès believes Edmond seeks revenge because she married Fernand but learns the truth when Edmond shows her Fernand's defamatory letter to Villefort. He tells her of the years of imprisonment that now require vengeance. She tells him of her prayers for him and of her horrible dreams for the ten years since she thought he died trying to escape from the Château d'If. When he vows that her son shall live, she confesses her undying love for "Edmond," says that she, too, has suffered, and that he is the noble man she remembers. Analysis of the metaphors: Edmond is the lion and the avenger, and Mercédès' sad, despairing reference to Edmond as her son's murderer breaks through Edmond's hardness, taming the lion and overcoming the avenger. Edmond is Death and the phantom. He believes he must die if Albert lives, and Death will return to its tomb and the phantom to darkness. pp. 456-462)*

5. Discuss the final confrontation between Monte Cristo and Fernand (Morcerf). Analyze the irony in this section. *(Fernand believes his son is a coward for backing out of the duel with Monte Cristo and challenges him to a duel. Fernand learns Monte Cristo's true identity, realizes Mercédès*

and Albert are abandoning him, and kills himself. Irony: Monte Cristo's knowledge of the truth during the veiled discussion between himself and Fernand, including guilt, the enemy, and prior acquaintance; Fernand's final recognition of and reaction to the reappearance of Edmond Dantès. pp. 470-475)

6. **Prediction:** Will Edmond and Mercédès have a chance at future happiness together?

Supplementary Activities

1. Note the metaphors: news of Fernand's treachery: flash of lightning; his response: thunderbolt (p. 436); Albert: mad dog (p. 447)

2. Have a student read Haydee's accusation of Fernand aloud as a monologue (pp. 440-444).

3. Note the symbolism of the opera the Count is watching when Albert challenges him to a duel. *("William Tell": Tell is a man of tremendous strengths who is arrested for refusing to bow to the hat of Gessler, who will allow Tell to go free if he can shoot an apple off his own son's head. Tell hits the apple and says he would have killed Gessler if the arrow had hurt his son. Tell eventually kills the tyrant. Symbolically, this speaks of the close bond between father and son and explains Albert's intense anger toward the Count [the tyrant] because of his unjust treatment of Fernand [the innocent]. p. 456)*

Chapters 60-62, pp. 476-499

Valentine becomes ill from poison and Maximilian goes to Monte Cristo for help. Monte Cristo, disguised as the Italian priest Busoni, attempts to save Valentine. Valentine recognizes Mme. de Villefort as her would-be murderer.

Vocabulary

panacea (477)	paroxysm (482)	implacable (484)	somnolence (489)
stupefaction (491)	diabolical (493)	efface (495)	indiscreet (495)

Discussion Questions

1. Examine the poisoning of Valentine: her grandfather's foresight, her near-death experience, Maximilian's role, Monte Cristo's role. Note Monte Cristo's initial reaction and his change of heart. *(Noirtier, foreseeing that Valentine will be the next victim, has had her taking some of his medicine, which contains brucine, each day to build her immunity. She ingests enough of the poison, placed in sugared water, to cause a seizure and appears near death. Maximilian, who is with her, goes to Monte Cristo for help, who tells Maximilian that God's justice has fallen on Villefort's house. When Maximilian reveals his love for Valentine, Monte Cristo, stricken with grief, assures him that Valentine will not die. Monte Cristo moves next door to the Villeforts, using the alias Signor Busoni, an Italian priest. He appears to Valentine, who is weak from the attack, reveals that he has watched over her for four nights, and has substituted a health-giving potion for her drink, which has been poisoned. He helps her detect the would-be murderer, Mme. de Villefort, then explains and initiates his plan to save her by giving her a powerful narcotic. pp. 476-490)*

2. Analyze the metaphor comparing Monte Cristo to a wounded lion, the simile comparing him to a fallen angel, the allusion to being bitten by the serpent, and the simile comparing his face to a sleeping child. *(When he hears of Maximilian's love for Valentine, Monte Cristo roars like a wounded lion, indicating great agony. He acknowledges that he watched indifferently as the tragedy [deaths by poison] unfolded, then laughed like a fallen angel at evil. He feels that the serpent [the devil] has bitten him with the desire for revenge. Allusion reference: Bible, Genesis 3: 1-5. After the mental battle, his face is as calm as that of a sleeping child for he has come to peace with his desire for revenge and has formulated a plan to save Valentine. pp. 483-484)*

3. **Prediction:** How does Monte Cristo plan to save Valentine? Will he be successful?

Supplementary Activity

As a class, create the dialogue between the angel of light and the angel of darkness as they speak to Monte Cristo (see page 484). Have two students stage the dialogue.

Chapters 63-66, pp. 499-528

The doctor announces Valentine's death and detects poison in her glass. Maximilian, consumed with grief, tells her father of their love. The Abbé Busoni comes to pray over Valentine. Villefort learns from Noirtier the name of the murderer. Monte Cristo reveals to the Morrels his identity as their benefactor. Monte Cristo completes his plan to ruin Danglars financially.

Vocabulary

imprecations (502)   ebullition (505)   affable (511)   tantamount (515)

Discussion Questions

1. Analyze Valentine's "death." Elicit student response as to whether or not she is dead and, if not, what will happen to her. Compare her "death" with that of Juliet in *Romeo and Juliet*. *(Mme. de Villefort believes she has poisoned Valentine and finds her cold and unresponsive. The doctor pronounces her dead by poisoning. Villefort is overwhelmed with grief. Maximilian arrives, believes Valentine is dead, and reveals their love for each other. Noirtier tells his son the name of the murderer, and Villefort vows to Maximilian and the doctor that he will avenge the deaths but begs them not to report the murder. The Abbé Busoni—actually Monte Cristo—is called to pray over Valentine and watches her throughout the night. Note that Noirtier peacefully sleeps, indicating his knowledge of Monte Cristo's intervention. pp. 499-511)*

2. Analyze the paradox of Mme. de Villefort's confidence and terror following Valentine's death. Note the simile, "[Mme. de Villefort]...looking like a statue of terror" (p. 502). *(She puts the poison into the tumbler by Valentine's bed, returns to find it three-fourths empty, empties the remaining contents, dries the tumbler, and places it on the table. She is confident that Valentine is dead and that her own part in the death will never be discovered. When she reenters the death room, the doctor is examining the tumbler, which is again one-fourth full with liquid the same color as that Mme. de Villefort had placed in it. When the doctor discovers the type of poison in the tumbler, Mme. de Villefort is terror stricken, staggers to the door, disappears, and faints. pp. 500-503)*

3. Examine the events in Danglars' life, Monte Cristo's visit to him, and the ensuing events. Note the prophetic tone of Danglars' statement, "He who wishes harm to others shall himself suffer misfortune" (p. 511). *(Andrea de Cavalcanti, to whom Eugénie Danglars was betrothed, has proven to be an imposter and has been arrested. Monte Cristo claims the remainder of his credit from Danglars, five million francs, exactly the amount Danglars holds on deposit from the hospitals. Just as Monte Cristo is leaving Danglars, the hospital treasurer arrives to redeem the bonds. Facing complete financial ruin and disgrace, Danglars asks for and receives a reprieve of a few hours. He hastily makes plans to leave the country; Prophetic: Danglars, who was instrumental in Fernand's ruin, now faces disgrace. pp. 511-517)*

4. Analyze Maximilian's despair. Compare Monte Cristo's intervention in Maximilian's life with his role in the elder Morrel's life. Note the commonality of bankruptcy today. Elicit student response to the honor of suicide in 19th-century France and the dishonor of suicide today. Discuss alternatives for those who might consider suicide, i.e., talking to parents or a counselor to find help, suicide crisis hotline, etc. *(Maximilian, distraught over Valentine's death, is writing a suicide note, with his pistols beside him. Maximilian accuses Monte Cristo of deceiving him with hopes of saving Valentine. Monte Cristo reveals that he is the benefactor who once saved the elder Morrel's life. Overcome with gratitude, Maximilian promises Monte Cristo he will not take his own life. Maximilian's father, who faced bankruptcy and dishonor, was also writing a suicide note and had pistols prepared when "Sinbad the Sailor" [Dantès] saved his business and his life. pp. 170-173, 519-525)*

5. Note the foreshadowing of Monte Cristo's words and actions: hidden future and a day when Maximilian will thank Monte Cristo for saving his life, Monte Cristo's smile in response to Maximilian's comment about seeing Valentine again, Monte Cristo's directive to hope and his promise of a remedy in one month, God's ability to perform miracles, and the departure of Haydee (pp. 526-528). *(The foreshadowing is fulfilled in Chapter 71.)*

6. **Prediction:** What does the future hold for Monte Cristo? for Maximilian and Valentine? for Haydee?

Supplementary Activities

1. As a class or individually, write a five-senses poem for Hope.

2. Note the literary devices: **Similes**—Danglars' wealth like the Pyramids (p. 512); Danglars...stretched out his hand as the vulture stretches out its claw (p. 514); [Julie's] two bright tears of joy coursed down her cheeks like two drops of morning dew (p. 524) **Allusions**—Croesus (p. 513): last king of Lydia (now western Turkey), under whose rule the country achieved vast wealth through gold mining and trade; daughter of Jairus (p. 526): Mark 5:22-24, 35-43; walk upon the waves like the apostle (p. 527): Matthew 14:29; faith to move mountains (p. 527): Matthew 17:20.

Chapters 67-69, pp. 528-556

Danglars has fled. Mme. Danglars is rich but rejected by Debray. Mercédès and Albert live in near-poverty. Villefort accuses his wife of murdering four people, and she kills their son Edward and herself, driving Villefort to insanity.

Vocabulary

opulence (533) ostentatious (534) tacitly (535) assizes (542)
expiation (550)

Discussion Questions

1. Examine the revelations in the meeting between Mme. Danglars and Lucien Debray. *(They have been meeting clandestinely for some time and have been lovers as well as business partners. At their final meeting, she tells him that her husband has left. He reads Danglars farewell letter and learns that he blames his wife for his financial ruin, and that he leaves her rich but with little honor. Mme. Danglars believes Debray will now marry her, but he rejects her and advises her to travel. pp. 528-534)*

2. Discuss the living conditions of Mercédès and Albert. *(They have been reduced from luxury to near poverty. They have both changed, losing their spark for life. Albert plans to use his remaining money for them to go to Marseilles to retrieve the three thousand francs Monte Cristo told him were buried there for them. Albert plans to enter the military and arrange for his mother to live at Marseilles until he returns. Note the reference to a man watching them as they leave for Marseilles. pp. 534-541)*

3. Analyze Mme. de Villefort's "trial," her judge, and the punishment. Note the foreshadowing in Villefort's statement, "You must have kept some poison...to save you from the punishment you deserve!" (p. 548) and in her desperate words, "I kill my son!" (p. 550). *(Mme. de Villefort is playing with Edward, and Villefort sends him from the room, then confronts his wife. Acting as her judge, he accuses her of the poisoning deaths and vows to make her crimes public and to sentence her to death on the scaffold unless she has kept enough poison to kill herself. Mme. de Villefort falls to her knees and begs for her life for the sake of their love and their child. He leaves her with the promise of public denouncement and arrest if she still lives when he returns. As he drives home after a day at court, he decides that his wife must live, repent, and raise their son, but that she and Edward must leave to avoid public disgrace. She greets him, already in the throe of death, and Villefort finds Edward dead, killed by his mother. pp. 546-553)*

4. Analyze the scene between Abbé Busoni and Villefort. *(The abbé [Monte Cristo] is in Noirtier's room when Villefort enters following the deaths of his wife and child. "Busoni" tells him he can now pray for God to forgive Villefort because the retribution is sufficient. He reveals his true identity and reminds Villefort of the crimes he committed against Dantès. Dantès realizes his vengeance has gone too far when he sees Edward's body, and he tries desperately but vainly to revive him. The child's death and Villefort's consequent insanity cause Dantès to doubt whether or not he has had the right to seek and destroy his enemies. pp. 553-556)*

5. **Prediction:** What does Monte Cristo mean by, "Let me save the last one!"?

Supplementary Activities

1. Have students write a metaphor or simile for Regret.

2. Note the similes: Mercédès was like a queen who had stepped from her palace into a hut (p. 535); hollyhocks stood like ghosts of flowers (p. 542); fingers damp and red as though dipped in blood (p. 544); [Villefort] had become like a tiger wounded unto death; jumped over his wife's body as though it were a yawning furnace of red-hot coals (p. 553)

Chapters 70-71, pp. 556-580

Monte Cristo comes to get Maximilian and to say farewell to Julie and Emmanuel. Mercédès and Monte Cristo (now as Edmond Dantès) meet for the last time, expressing their failures and their sorrows to each other. Maximilian is reunited with Valentine on the Isle of Monte Cristo. Haydee declares her love for Monte Cristo, and they leave together.

Vocabulary

au revoir (567)   opalescent (570)   unctuous (574)

Discussion Questions

1. Analyze Mercédès and Edmond's final meeting. *(He finds her in the little garden in Marseilles where they had once been happy together. He offers her consolation as a friend and tells her Albert has chosen wisely and is a noble-hearted man. Edmond feels she would be justified in hating him, but she assures him that she cannot hate the man who saved her son's life. Rather, she hates and reproaches herself for her cowardice and feels that God has forsaken her, causing her to age with grief. She views Edmond as still handsome and dignified because God has sustained him. Edmond reveals his suffering in prison and the torment of his drive to exact vengeance on his enemies, causing him to become a wicked, treacherous man. Their final "au revoir" indicates their hope some day to meet again. Note Edmond's analysis of himself, "I felt myself pushed onward like a cloud of fire sent from Heaven to burn the cities of the wicked." pp. 563-567)*

2. Examine Monte Cristo's summation of his life and his rationale for telling his story. *(He tells Maximilian of a man [himself] who loved his father and set all his hopes on a woman whom he loved and was about to marry. The man was falsely accused and spent fourteen years in a dungeon and that he, like Maximilian, wanted to kill himself, but that God revealed himself through another human being. He miraculously left his "tomb," only to find his father dead and his fiancée faithless and married to one of his betrayers. Yet, the man has now found peace. He reveals the story to give Maximilian hope that his despair, too, will one day end. pp. 568-570)*

3. Summarize the final events in the denouement. *(Maximilian meets Monte Cristo on the Isle of Monte Cristo, who tells him he loves him as a son and will do anything to save him. Monte Cristo gives Maximilian a drug, which Maximilian believes will kill him. Instead, he goes into a deep sleep, thinks he is dead, and sees an angel that resembles Valentine. Maximilian and Valentine are reunited, and Monte Cristo gives them his property in Paris, where they will be reunited with Noirtier. Haydee, who accompanied Valentine to the island, says that she loves Monte Cristo and will kill herself if he leaves her. The love is mutual, and Monte Cristo realizes she is God's gift to him and that, through her, he can return to life. They sail away together. pp. 570-580)*

Supplementary Activities

1. Have students analyze the metaphors for death: "According as we have lived, death is either a friend who rocks us as gently as a nurse, or an enemy who violently tears the soul from the body" (p. 572).

2. As a class, compare Julie's analogy of her father and Abraham and her personification of Death. *(Her father, like Abraham [Bible, Genesis 22:1-14], was saved from Death by an angel; Morrel: Edmond Dantès with the bank notes and diamond; Abraham: an angel and a sacrificial ram)*

3. Have students write an analysis of Monte Cristo's parting words to Maximilian, "Tell the angel...to pray for a man who, like Satan, believed for one moment he was the equal of God, but who now acknowledges in all Christian humility that in God alone is supreme power and infinite wisdom" (p. 579).

Post-reading Discussion Questions

1. With students, develop a time line showing dates, setting, and events in Edmond Dantès' life. Include 1815 (Marseilles; Morrel, Danglars, Fernand, Villefort, Mercédès); 1815-1829 (Prisoner #37 imprisoned in Château d'If, Mercédès marries Fernand, Villefort rises in power, his father dies, etc.); 1820 (meets Abbé Faria, they plan escape); 1829 (escapes, finds treasure, returns to France and learns from Caderousse truth about imprisonment); 1838 (appears in Rome as Count of Monte Cristo, introduced to Parisian society); 1839 (conversation about the past between Mercédès and Edmond; see p. 460).

2. Complete and discuss the chart (see Supplementary Activity #1, Chapters 18-22) showing Dantès' pseudonyms and the characters with whom he interacts under that alias. Examine types of interaction and analyze the effectiveness of each alias. *(Dantès: his father, Villefort, Danglars, Fernand, Mercédès, Caderousse, Abbé Faria; Priest: Caderousse; Sinbad the Sailor: the Morrels; law clerk for Thomson and French: the Morrels, the inspector of prisons; Lord Wilmore: the Morrels; Doctor: Mme. de Villefort [discussion of poison]; Signor Busoni: Valentine and her family; the Count of Monte Cristo: Morcerf [Albert, Fernand, Mercédès], Danglars, Villefort family; Morrels, Haydee, etc.)*

3. Examine the roles of "father figures" in the novel: Abbé Faria/Edmond Dantès; the Count of Monte Cristo/Maximilian Morrel. Include the importance of giving hope, financial benefits, understanding of life and its consequences, etc.

4. Place a circle on the overhead transparency with the idiom, "The wheel has come full circle." Analyze how Dantès, through all of his aliases, comes full circle back to the man he was before betrayal, bitterness, and revenge. Note his reaction to Edward's death.

5. Analyze Dantès (as Monte Cristo) and his belief that he is God's instrument for revenge, noting especially two quotes from Dantès: "I, betrayed, assassinated, cast into a tomb, have risen from that tomb by the grace of God, and it is my duty to God to punish this man. He has sent me for that purpose and here I am" (p. 459); "Tell the angel...to pray for a man who, like Satan, believed for one moment he was the equal of God, but who now acknowledges in all Christian humility that in God alone is supreme power and infinite wisdom." Within the context of the novel, discuss the ramifications for anyone who places himself in God's role. (Note selections on pp. 457, 459, 555, 556, 565, 566, 579.)

6. Trace Dantès' (the Count of Monte Cristo's) path of revenge.

7. Analyze Dantès' final admonition to Maximilian, "...all human wisdom is contained in the words 'Wait and hope!'"

8. Bring scales to class such as those shown in the symbolic picture of Justice. Have available small weights (drapery weights are ideal). Discuss the good and bad deeds of the Count of Monte Cristo. For each deed, place a weight in the appropriate pan of the scales. Compare the results. *(Examples: Good: saving the Morrel family, rescuing Peppino and Albert, saving Valentine's life, buying Haydee from slavery; Bad: destroying Danglars and Villefort, giving Mme. de Villefort the poison, causing death of Edward.)*

9. Discuss the characters who symbolize: jealousy (Fernand), ambition (Danglars), greed (Mme. Danglars, Mme. de Villefort), self-promotion (Villefort, Debray), apathy (Caderousse), revenge (Dantès—the Count of Monte Cristo), innocence (Mercédès, Valentine, Julie), noble heart (Morrel, Abbé Faria, Noirtier), fraud (Cavalcantis), love (Haydee, Mercédès, Maximilian). Analyze how life's circumstances effect changes in the characters. *(Responses will vary. Ask students to justify their responses.)*

10. Analyze Dantès' statement, "Now, farewell to kindness, humanity, gratitude. Farewell to all the sentiments which rejoice the heart. I have played the part of Providence in recompensing the good, may the god of vengeance now permit me to punish the wicked" (p. 174). *(This, spoken just after Dantès has saved the Morrel family from ruin, indicates the point of change in the story. From this point on, he is bent on revenge.)*

11. Examine the familial relationships in the novel. *(Suggestions: Dantès/his father: loving, trusting, supportive; Morrel/his wife and children: protective, loving; Danglars/his wife and daughter: manipulative, at times unconcerned, mercenary; Fernand de Morcerf/Mercédès, Albert: manipulative, high expectations; Mercédès/Albert: tender, protective, loving; Albert toward Mercédès: affectionate almost to point of incestuous love; Villefort/his wife, Valentine, Edward: loves them but doesn't understand them; Mme. de Villefort toward Edward: protective, consumed with him.)*

Post-reading Extension Activities

Writing

1. Rewrite the story in a 24-line, iambic pentameter poem.

2. Write a summary of Dantès' life between the time he leaves France after talking to Caderousse and when he meets Albert and Franz in Rome (8 or 9 years).

3. Write a letter from Mercédès to Dantès just before she marries Fernand.

4. Write a short sequel showing what each of the following characters is doing five years after the novel ends: Mercédès, Albert, Maximilian and Valentine, Villefort, the Count of Monte Cristo, and Haydee.

Art

1. Design a coat-of-arms for Edmond Dantès as the Count of Monte Cristo.

2. Create a collage with half depicting vengeance and the other half mercy.

Current Events

Bring to class articles from newspapers or magazines with information about current alleged spies and the possible penalties they face if convicted. Compare Dantès' "trial" and imprisonment with the justice system today.

Drama

1. Write and present to the class a dialogue depicting the Count of Monte Cristo standing at the gate of heaven explaining to the angel why he should be allowed to enter.

2. Stage the final conversation between Dantès and Mercédès. Add appropriate background music.

Music

1. Write and perform a ballad that tells of the thwarted love of Dantès and Mercédès.

2. Bring to class and play selected recordings of music to express the mood of the novel. Explain your choices.

Viewing

View one of the movies of *The Count of Monte Cristo*. Play selected clips from the movie as you discuss the similarities and differences between the novel and the movie.

Assessment for *The Count of Monte Cristo*

Assessment is an ongoing process. The following ten items can be completed during the novel study. Once finished, the student and teacher will check the work. Points may be added to indicate the level of understanding.

Name _____ Date _____

Student   **Teacher**

_____   _____   1. Group work: The teacher will assign your group a specific section of the novel. On slips of paper, write five review questions over that section. After placing the questions in a basket, each person will draw one question and answer it during an oral review.

_____   _____   2. As the teacher calls out specific characteristics such as "greed," write the name of the person in the novel you think best matches the trait.

_____   _____   3. Display your extension project on the assigned day. Be prepared to explain your project.

_____   _____   4. Correct any quizzes or exams taken over the novel.

_____   _____   5. Write a précis of the book using at least ten of the vocabulary words you learned in the novel.

_____   _____   6. Compare any activities such as character charts and story maps in small groups of three or four.

_____   _____   7. Write an example of a metaphor and a simile.

_____   _____   8. Write a recommendation to a friend asking him or her to read the novel.

_____   _____   9. Write a two-line description of one of the characters but omit the name. Exchange with a partner and identify the character s/he has described.

_____   _____   10. Write a bio-poem about Dantès before or after he becomes the Count of Monte Cristo. Pattern—Line 1: name; Line 2: four of his traits; Line 3: designation (son, ally...); Line 4: feels...; Line 5: needs...; Line 6: gives...; Line 7: fears...; Line 8: regrets...; Line 9: destiny (in the book).

Glossary

Chapters 1-4, pp. 1-29

1. melancholy (1): sadness, gloom; tendency to be sad

2. imperceptibly (3): slightly, gradually

3. obsequious (3): polite or obedient from hope of gain or from fear; servile, fawning

4. vexation (15): irritation, exasperation, annoyance

5. imperious (17): haughty or arrogant

Chapters 5-7, pp. 29-49

1. usurpers (29): those who seize and hold power or authority by force

2. royalists (30): supporters of a king or royal government, especially in times of war or rebellion; supporters of Bourbons in France since 1793

3. plebeian (31): belonging to or having to do with the common people; the populace

4. imprudence (39): indiscretion, rashness; lack of wisdom before acting

5. presentiment (44): feeling or impression that something, especially something evil, is about to happen; vague sense of approaching misfortune

Chapters 8-13, pp. 50-91

1. compunction (52): uneasiness of mind because of wrongdoing; pricking of conscience; remorse

2. benevolence (64): desire to promote happiness of others; good will; kindly feeling; act of kindness

3. despotic (77): of a despot (monarch having absolute rule); having unlimited power; tyrannical

4. infamy (82): very bad reputation; public disgrace

5. prodigious (85): very great, huge, vast

6. cataleptic (88): unconscious with muscles becoming rigid

Chapters 14-17, pp. 91-122

1. requiem (107): Mass for the dead; anything that suggests a service or hymn for the dead

2. torpid (113): dull, inactive, sluggish

3. misanthropy (119): hatred, dislike; distrust of people

4. chimerical (120): unreal, imaginary, absurd, impossible

Chapters 18-22, pp. 122-150

1. rendezvous (122): an appointment to meet at a fixed place or time

2. labyrinth (124): a number of connecting passages so arranged that it is hard to find one's way from one point to another; maze

3. intrepid (128): very brave; fearless; courageous, dauntless

4. ironical (138): expressing one thing and meaning the opposite

5. conscription (145): compulsory internment of men in the armed services

Chapters 23-25, pp. 150-174

1. inveterate (155): confirmed in habit, practice, or feeling; habitual

2. probity (159): high principle; uprightness; honesty

3. verity (164): truth

4. repugnance (167): strong dislike, distaste, or aversion

Chapters 26-29, pp. 174-217

1. cicerone (175): guide for sightseers who explains artifacts or curiosities of places

2. dissertations (184): formal discussions of a subject

3. alacrity (206): brisk and eager action; prompt, cheerful willingness

4. catacombs (208): underground gallery forming a burial place; network of galleries with recesses to bury the dead

Chapters 30-33, pp. 218-256

1. philanthropic (223): charitable; benevolent; kindly

2. cosmopolitan (226): belonging to all parts of the world; feeling at home in any part of the world

3. prosaic (230): matter-of-fact; ordinary, commonplace, or dull

4. antipathy (235): strong or fixed dislike; aversion

5. importunate (239): asking repeatedly; persistent; urgent

6. perspicacious (240): keen in observing and understanding; discerning

7. filial (242): of a son or daughter; due from son or daughter toward mother or father

Chapters 34-37, pp. 257-283

1. sonorous (258): giving out or having a deep, vibrant, ringing sound

2. pseudonym (265): assumed name; alias

3. toxicology (267): science that deals with poisons and their effects, detection, and antidotes

4. taciturn (268): saying very little; inclined to silence

5. candid (280): saying openly what one really thinks; outspoken

Chapters 38-42, pp. 284-320

1. avaricious (287): greedy; greatly desiring money or property

2. notary (297): public officer authorized to certify deeds and contracts and to attend to legal matters

3. approbation (298): favorable opinion; approval

4. propriety (303): quality or condition of being proper

5. patriarch (306): father or ruler of a family or tribe

6. pecuniary (307): of or having to do with money

7. nabob (319): native ruler in India; an important person

8. conjugal (320): of or having to do with marriage

Chapters 43-46, pp. 320-353

1. presages (327): signs felt as warnings; omens

2. sardonic (330): bitterly contemptuous; coldly scornful; mocking

3. condescension (334): haughty or patronizing attitude

4. eccentric (338): out of the ordinary; peculiar; odd

5. banalities (340): commonplace, trite statements

6. decorum (349): proper behavior; good taste in conduct, speech, or dress

7. apoplectic (352): sudden loss or lessening of the power to feel, think, or move; stroke

Chapters 47-49, pp. 353-394

1. dispassionately (356): free from emotion or prejudice; calmly; impartially

2. ineffable (359): too great to be described in words

3. austere (368): stern in manner or appearance; harsh

4. adherent (379): faithful supporter; follower

5. reparation (383): compensation for wrong or injury done

6. dexterity (389): manual skill; neatness

Chapters 50-53, pp. 394-434

1. contemptuous (399): scornful; showing contempt

2. injunction (401): command, order

3. firman (409): an order issued by an Oriental ruler

4. hashish (412): dried flowers, top leaves, tender parts of Indian hemp prepared for use as a narcotic; marijuana

5. cryptic (417): having a hidden meaning; secretive; mysterious

6. calumnies (418): false statements made on purpose to harm someone; slander

7. incessant (430): never ending; continual

8. phenomena (431): facts, events, or circumstances that can be observed; signs, manifestations

9. flagrant (432): glaringly offensive; notorious; outrageous; scandalous

Chapters 54-59, pp. 434-475

1. defamatory (435): slanderous or libelous

2. compatriots (438): fellow countrymen

3. cognizant: (446): aware; observant

4. odious (459): very displeasing; hateful; offensive

5. apparition (474): supernatural sight or thing; ghost; phantom

Chapters 60-62, pp. 476-499

1. panacea (477): remedy for all disease or ills; cure-all

2. paroxysm (482): severe, sudden attack

3. implacable (484): refusing to be reconciled; unyielding; unforgiving

4. somnolence (489): sleepiness; drowsiness

5. stupefaction (491): dazed or senseless condition

6. diabolical (493): devilish; evil; action aided by the devil

7. efface (495): rub out; destroy

8. indiscreet (495): not wise and judicious; imprudent

Chapters 63-66, pp. 499-528

1. imprecations (502): acts of calling down evil, curses, or calamity on a person

2. ebullition (505): outburst; boiling or bubbling up

3. affable (511): easy to talk to; courteous; gracious

4. tantamount (515): equivalent

Chapters 67-69, pp. 528-556

1. opulence (533): wealth; riches

2. ostentatious (534): done for display; intended to attract notice

3. tacitly (535): implied or understood without being openly expressed

4. assizes (542): sessions of a law court

5. expiation (550): making amends for a sin, wrong, or crime; atonement

Chapters 70-71, pp. 556-580

1. *au revoir* (567): good-bye until we see each other again

2. opalescent (570): having a change of colors like that of an opal

3. unctuous (574): like an oil or ointment; soothing

Notes

The Count of Monte Cristo
Alexandre Dumas

Activities to teach
Reading
Thinking
and
Writing

Novel Units® Teacher Guides and Student Packets

SP indicates Student Packet for this title.   * Fall 2001 title   • Spring 2002 title

THE COUNT OF MONTE CRISTO

by
Alexandre Dumas

Student Packet

Written by
Pat Watson

Contains masters for:

2	Prereading Activities
5	Vocabulary Activities
1	Study Guide (7 pages)
5	Literary Analysis Activities
3	Comprehension Activities
5	Unit Quizzes
2	Final Tests (Two Levels)

PLUS   Detailed Answer Key

Note

The Tor paperback edition of the book, abridged, published by Tom Doherty Associates, LLC, ©1998, was used to prepare this guide. Page references may differ in other editions.

Please note: Please assess the appropriateness of this book for the age level and maturity of your students prior to reading and discussing it with your class.

ISBN 1-58130-713-6

To order, contact your local school supply store, or—

Novel Units, Inc.
P.O. Box 791610
San Antonio, TX 78279

Web site: www.educyberstor.com

Name _____

Directions: Rate each of the following statements before you read the novel and discuss your ratings with a partner. After you have completed the novel, rate and discuss the statements again.

1———— 2———— 3 ———— 4 ———— 5 ———— 6

agree strongly   strongly disagree

	Before	**After**
1. Family loyalty supercedes political loyalty.	_____	_____
2. False imprisonment justifies revenge.	_____	_____
3. A person who loves another will wait for his or her "true love" as long as it takes.	_____	_____
4. Outward success indicates inner peace.	_____	_____
5. Love is stronger than hate.	_____	_____
6. Honorable men always pay their debts.	_____	_____
7. Vengeance harms the avenger as much as his victim.	_____	_____
8. Immense wealth alleviates the pain of past injustices.	_____	_____
9. "Money talks" is an accurate adage.	_____	_____
10. The satisfaction of revenge justifies the means by which it is attained.	_____	_____
11. Most of us hide behind a "mask" of some kind.	_____	_____
12. Fate (what will be, will be) controls our destiny.	_____	_____

Name _____

Getting the "Lay of the Land"

Directions: Prepare for reading by answering the following short-answer questions.

1. Who is the author?

   _____

2. What does the title suggest to you about the book?

   _____

   _____

   _____

   _____

3. When was the book written?

   _____

4. How many pages are there in the book?

   _____

5. Thumb through the book. Read three pages—one from near the beginning, one from near the middle, and one from near the end. What predictions do you make about the book?

   _____

   _____

   _____

   _____

   _____

6. What does the cover suggest to you about the book?

   _____

   _____

   _____

   _____

Name _____

melancholy (1)	imperceptibly (3)	obsequious (3)	vexation (15)
imperious (17)	usurpers (29)	royalists (30)	plebeian (31)
imprudence (39)	presentiment (44)	compunction (52)	benevolence (64)
despotic (77)	infamy (82)	prodigious (85)	cataleptic (88)
requiem (107)	torpid (113)	misanthropy (119)	chimerical (120)

Directions: Match each vocabulary word with the correct definition.

_____ 1. melancholy   a. act of kindness

_____ 2. imperceptibly   b. service for the dead

_____ 3. obsequious   c. having to do with the common people

_____ 4. vexation   d. rigid muscles due to a seizure

_____ 5. imperious   e. tendency to be sad

_____ 6. usurpers   f. imaginary or absurd

_____ 7. royalists   g. regret or remorse

_____ 8. plebeian   h. servile, fawning

_____ 9. imprudence   i. very bad reputation

_____ 10. presentiment   j. dull and inactive

_____ 11. compunction   k. irritation or annoyance

_____ 12. benevolence   l. vague sense of approaching misfortune

_____ 13. despotic   m. those who seize and hold power by force

_____ 14. infamy   n. slightly, gradually

_____ 15. prodigious   o. of a tyrannical, absolute ruler

_____ 16. cataleptic   p. haughty or arrogant

_____ 17. requiem   q. supporters of a king

_____ 18. torpid   r. hatred or distrust of people

_____ 19. misanthropy   s. indiscretion or rashness

_____ 20. chimerical   t. huge or vast

Name _____

The Count of Monte Cristo
Activity #4 • Vocabulary
Chapters 18-33

rendezvous (122)	labyrinth (124)	intrepid (128)	ironical (138)
conscription (145)	inveterate (155)	probity (159)	verity (164)
repugnance (167)	cicerone (175)	dissertations (184)	alacrity (206)
catacombs (208)	philanthropic (223)	cosmopolitan (226)	prosaic (230)
antipathy (235)	importunate (239)	perspicacious (240)	filial (242)

Directions: Match each word with the word or phrase that means the *opposite*.

_____ 1. rendezvous

_____ 2. labyrinth

_____ 3. intrepid

_____ 4. ironical

_____ 5. conscription

_____ 6. inveterate

_____ 7. probity

_____ 8. verity

_____ 9. repugnance

_____ 10. cicerone

_____ 11. dissertations

_____ 12. alacrity

_____ 13. catacombs

_____ 14. philanthropic

_____ 15. cosmopolitan

_____ 16. prosaic

_____ 17. antipathy

_____ 18. importunate

_____ 19. perspicacious

_____ 20. filial

a. fabrication

b. unsophisticated

c. lethargy

d. random meeting

e. fascinating

f. straightforward

g. disrespectful toward parents

h. one who is escorted

i. not firmly established

j. love

k. open countryside

l. straight path

m. dishonesty

n. irresolute

o. fearful

p. unobservant

q. refusal to comment

r. voluntary military service

s. compatibility

t. uncharitable

sonorous (258)	pseudonyms (265)	toxicology (267)	taciturn (268)
candid (280)	avaricious (287)	notary (297)	approbation (298)
propriety (303)	patriarch (306)	pecuniary (307)	nabob (319)
conjugal (320)	presages (327)	sardonic (330)	condescension (334)
eccentric (338)	banalities (340)	decorum (349)	apoplectic (352)

Directions: In the chart below, (1) place a check mark in the column that best describes your familiarity with the word; (2) find the sentence in which the word appears in the text of the novel; (3) look up each word in the dictionary to find the definition as used in the novel.

Vocabulary Word	I Can Define	I Have Seen/Heard	New Word For Me
1. sonorous (258)			
2. pseudonyms (265)			
3. toxicology (267)			
4. taciturn (268)			
5. candid (280)			
6. avaricious (287)			
7. notary (297)			
8. approbation (298)			
9. propriety (303)			
10. patriarch (306)			
11. pecuniary (307)			
12. nabob (319)			
13. conjugal (320)			
14. presages (327)			
15. sardonic (330)			
16. condescension (334)			
17. eccentric (338)			
18. banalities (340)			
19. decorum (349)			
20. apoplectic (352)			

dispassionately (356)	ineffable (359)	austere (368)	adherent (379)
reparation (383)	dexterity (389)	contemptuous (399)	injunction (401)
firman (409)	hashish (412)	cryptic (417)	calumnies (418)
incessant (430)	phenomena (431)	flagrant (432)	defamatory (435)
compatriots (438)	cognizant (446)	odious (459)	apparition (474)

Directions: Fill in the blanks in the following sentences with the correct vocabulary word. Refer to the word on the page on which it is found in the novel for applicability.

1. Albert de Morcerf views himself as a(n) _____ scholar of Plato.

2. The Count of Monte Cristo carries _____ inside an emerald box.

3. Maximilian Morrel believes that Valentine views her impending marriage to Franz

   _____ .

4. The doctor, M. d'Avrigny, is concerned about the _____ deaths in the Villefort household.

5. Danglars is _____ of the fact that the Count of Morcerf has been convicted of treason.

6. Noirtier's countenance reflects a(n) _____, noble expression.

7. The Count of Monte Cristo issues a(n) _____ to Haydee to reveal her father's fate.

8. The doctor who tends to the patients in Villefort's house insinuates that the deaths are caused by _____ within the family.

9. Danglars insinuates that _____ have been spoken against the Morcerfs.

10. Fernand views Edmond Dantès as a(n) _____ who reappears to destroy him.

11. The newspaper article prints _____ information about the Count of Morcerf.

12. Maximilian Morrel expresses _____ gratitude for Valentine's love.

13. A duel in early 19th-century France was viewed as a means of _____.

14. The Sultan issued a(n) _____ for Ali Tebelin's execution.

15. The Count of Morcerf tells the court of inquiry that he is the only one of his _____ to survive the war in which Ali Tebelin died.

16. The Count of Monte Cristo tells Mercédès that Fernand's actions have been _____.

17. The doctor accuses Valentine of committing a(n) _____ crime.

18. The captain of the *Pharaon* had been a loyal _____ of Napoleon.

19. Danglars demonstrates _____ in closing a door.

20. The Count of Monte Cristo is not deceived by Danglars' _____ remarks.

panacea (477)   paroxysm (482)   implacable (484)   somnolence (489)
stupefaction (491)   diabolical (493)   efface (495)   indiscreet (495)
imprecations (502)   ebullition (505)   affable (511)   tantamount (515)
opulence (533)   ostentatious (534)   tacitly (535)   assizes (542)
expiation (550)   *au revoir* (567)   opalescent (570)   unctuous (575)

Directions: Your teacher will assign you one word from the list above. Turn to the page where the word appears in the novel and examine how it is used in context. Complete the word map for your word and explain the finished map to the class.

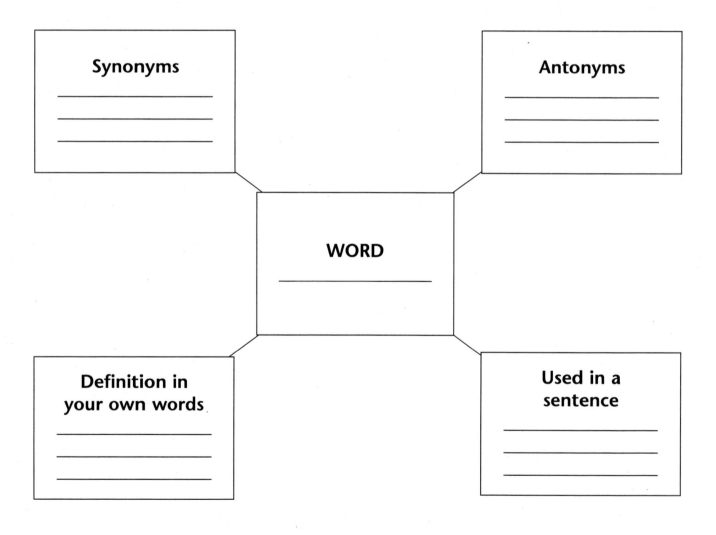

Synonyms

Antonyms

WORD

Definition in your own words

Used in a sentence

Directions: Answer the following questions on separate paper. The starred questions indicate thought or opinion or an activity. Use the answers in class discussions, for writing assignments, and to review for tests.

Chapters 1-4

1. Identify the following: Edmond Dantès, Danglars, Morrel, Caderousse, Fernand, Mercédès.

2. Explain what happened to the captain of the *Pharaon* prior to its arrival in France. What effect does this have on Dantès?

3. *Explain why each of the following men conspires against Dantès: Danglars, Caderousse, Fernand. Who do you think is the "ringleader" in this conspiracy? Why?

4. *What happens to Dantès at the betrothal feast? Why? What do you think his fate will be?

5. *Prediction: What will happen to Mercédès and to Dantès' father?

6. *Activity: Bring to class current newspaper or magazine articles relating to accused or convicted spies.

Chapters 5-7

1. *Identify Villefort and explain his relationship to Noirtier. Why is this important to the plot? Explain why you do or do not think Villefort is justified in his feelings toward Noirtier.

2. Describe Villefort's inquisition of Dantès. What is Villefort's initial reaction to Dantès and why does he change? What is Villefort's final decision?

3. *Identify the Château d'If. Quote two of the similes that describe the Château d'If and Dantès' reaction to it.

4. *Prediction: What will happen to Dantès?

5. *Activity: Write a metaphor or simile poem that describes Dantès' terror. Pattern: Line 1: noun (also the title); Lines 2-4: something about the subject with each line describing the subject in a different way; Line 5: metaphor or simile that begins with the noun from line 1.

Chapters 8-13

1. *Why does Mercédès visit Villefort? How does he react? What might have changed the outcome of her visit?

2. How do the following characters react to Dantès' imprisonment: Mercédès, Fernand, M. Morrel, Caderousse, Danglars, Dantès' father?

3. Explain the political upheaval in France. How does Villefort promote himself during this time?

4. *How does Dantès react to prison life? What changes his despair to hope? What do you think this indicates?

5. Identify the abbé and explain his effect on Dantès.

6. *Prediction: Will Dantès and the abbé escape the Château d'If?

7. *Activity: Research the Reign of Terror and be prepared to share your information during a class discussion.

Chapters 14-17

1. What does the abbé reveal to Dantès about the Isle of Monte Cristo? Why does he do so?

2. *How does Dantès escape from Château d'If? Who rescues him? Explain why you think this is or is not plausible.

3. *How long has Dantès been in prison? How has he changed during this time?

4. *Prediction: Will Dantès find the treasure? If so, how will it change his life?

5. *Activity: Write a short poem that reflects Dantès' feeling of being totally alone after the abbé dies.

6. *Activity: Draw a map to the hidden treasure on the Isle of Monte Cristo.

Chapters 18-22

1. Why does Dantès pretend to be injured on the Isle of Monte Cristo?

2. What does Dantès find on the Isle of Monte Cristo? How does he do so?

3. *Explain the disguise under which Dantès returns to France. Why do you think he does so?

4. How does Dantès get Caderousse to reveal information? What does Dantès discover from him?

5. *Prediction: What do you think Dantès will do with the information he has received?

6. *Activity: Write a name poem for Caderousse. Pattern: place the letters of his name vertically on the paper; for each letter, write a word or a phrase that describes him or tells something about him.

7. *Activity: Begin a list of the pseudonyms Dantès uses. Opposite each alias, write the name(s) of the characters he encounters using that disguise.

Chapters 23-25

1. Identify the pseudonyms under which Dantès appears in this section. Explain the importance of each one.

2. *What does Dantès find out from the prison records? Who signed the order for his imprisonment? What do you think he will do now?

3. What has happened to Morrel since Dantès left? What does Dantès do?

4. *Prediction: What does Dantès mean by his "farewell" to kindness, humanity, and gratitude?

5. *Activity: Draw a caricature of Sinbad the Sailor.

Chapters 26-29

1. Describe the Count of Monte Cristo.

2. *Whom does Monte Cristo meet in Rome? Why do you think this is important to the plot?

3. What happens to Albert de Morcerf? What does Monte Cristo do for him? What does he ask of Albert?

4. *Prediction: Quote Franz's premonition about Monte Cristo's visit to Paris and explain what you think this means.

5. *Activity: Bring to class pictures of Rome.

6. *Activity: Research and be prepared to discuss public executions of 19th-century European countries.

Chapters 30-33

1. Whom does Monte Cristo meet when he visits the Morcerf home?

2. What does Monte Cristo learn about Fernand?

3. *How does Mercédès react to Monte Cristo? What does she tell Albert about him? How would you explain her reaction?

4. *What is Danglars' profession? Why is this important to the plot?

5. *What happens involving the Danglars' dappled gray horses? Why do you think this is significant?

6. *Activity: Write a cinquain poem, "Dame Fortune," based on Monte Cristo's personification of Fortune (p. 237). Pattern: Line 1: title; Line 2: two words to describe the title; Line 3: three words to express action concerning the title; Line 4: four words to express feelings about the title; Line 5: a synonym for the title.

7. *Activity: Draw a caricature of Danglars based on Monte Cristo's metaphor of him: snake, vulture, buzzard (p. 243).

Chapters 34-37

1. Identify Haydee.

2. *What does Monte Cristo discover when he visits Maximilian Morrel? Explain the irony in the conversation.

3. *Identify and describe the people Monte Cristo encounters in the Villefort home. What do he and Mme. de Villefort discuss? Why do you think this is important?

4. Whom does Monte Cristo plan to invite for dinner at his home? Whom does he plan to exclude?

5. *Prediction: What will happen in the betrothals of Valentine de Villefort to Franz d'Épinay and Eugénie Danglars to Albert de Morcerf?

6. *Activity: Research the role of Lady Macbeth in Shakespeare's *Macbeth* and explain why you think the author alludes to her.

Chapters 38-42

1. Explain how the characters from Monte Cristo's past interweave in this section.

2. How do each of the following feel about Valentine's impending marriage to Franz: Valentine, her father, Mme. de Villefort, Noirtier?

3. *What is Noirtier's solution to the marriage? Do you think he will be successful?

4. *What happens that damages Danglars financially? Explain why you do or do not think Monte Cristo was instrumental in the loss.

5. *Who are the Cavalcantis? What role do you think they will play in Monte Cristo's revenge?

6. *Activity: Write an acrostic for Revenge.

Chapters 43-46

1. *Summarize the "conjugal" conversation between Danglars and his wife. What role do you think Debray plays in their lives?

2. What does Danglars tell Monte Cristo about Morcerf? What does Monte Cristo suggest to Danglars concerning Morcerf (Fernand)?

3. Summarize the conversation between the Count of Monte Cristo and Mercédès.

4. Who is Saint-Méran and what happens to him?

5. *Prediction: What has really happened to Saint-Méran and how will this affect the plot?

6. *Activity: Write a five-senses poem about Greed. Pattern: Line 1: color of the emotion; Line 2: sound of the emotion; Line 3: taste of the emotion; Line 4: smell of the emotion; Line 5: sight (what the emotion looks like); Line 6: feeling evoked by the emotion.

Chapters 47-49

1. How does Valentine react when Maximilian begs her to elope with him?

2. *What does Doctor d'Avrigny tell Villefort? How do you think this will change the story line?

3. *Explain the role Noirtier plays in Valentine's life. What information does he reveal to Franz? What do you think Franz will do now?

4. What does Danglars tell Monte Cristo he has discovered about Fernand?

5. *Prediction: What has Danglars discovered about Fernand and Janina?

6. *Activity: Research the poison brucine (strychnine): type, derivative, legal uses, symptoms of ingestion, treatment. Be prepared to discuss this with the class.

Chapters 50-53

1. *What does Haydee reveal about her past? Why do you think Monte Cristo cautions Albert against mentioning his father's name?

2. What does Danglars tell Morcerf when Danglars comes to discuss the engagement of Albert and Eugénie?

3. What happens to Barrios? What does the doctor imply to Villefort? How does Villefort react?

4. *Prediction: Will there be other deaths? If so, who will die?

5. *Activity: Write a metaphor poem for Betrayal.

Chapters 54-59

1. Describe what happens at Morcerf's trial. What is the turning point? Why?

2. *Why does Albert challenge Monte Cristo to a duel? Explain why you do or do not think Albert's actions are justified.

3. Why does Mercédès come to see Monte Cristo? What is the result of her visit?

4. *Explain what Monte Cristo means when he says, "Death will return to its tomb, the phantom to darkness!" (p. 461)

5. *Activity: Research the opera "William Tell" and explain the symbolism to the story line.

Chapters 60-62

1. Explain what happens to Valentine. How has her grandfather been protecting her?

2. *What happens when Maximilian goes to Monte Cristo for help? What breaks through the hardness of Monte Cristo's heart? How does he then react?

3. What does Monte Cristo do for Valentine?

4. *Prediction: How does Monte Cristo plan to save Valentine? Will he be successful?

16

Chapters 63-66

1. *What happens to Valentine? Do you think Monte Cristo has failed in his promise to Maximilian? Why or why not?

2. Why does Mme. de Villefort react in terror when she enters Valentine's room?

3. What is Monte Cristo's final act of vengeance on Danglars?

4. *How does Monte Cristo prevent Maximilian's suicide? Do you think Maximilian will try again?

5. *Prediction: What does the future hold for Monte Cristo? for Maximilian and Valentine? for Haydee?

6. *Activity: Write a five-senses poem for Hope.

Chapters 67-69

1. What does this section reveal about Mme. Danglars and Lucien Debray?

2. What are the plans of Albert and Mercédès? What arrangements has Monte Cristo made to help them?

3. Describe Mme. de Villefort's "trial" and her punishment. Who is the innocent victim?

4. *How does Monte Cristo at first view his final vengeance against Villefort? What causes him to change?

5. *Activity: Write a metaphor or simile for Regret.

Chapters 70-71

1. Describe Edmond and Mercédès' final meeting. How does Mercédès view herself? How does she view Edmond?

2. What happens to the following characters in the denouement: Maximilian, Valentine, Monte Cristo, Haydee?

3. *Activity: Write a short analysis of Monte Cristo's parting words to Maximilian, "...a man who, like Satan, believed for one moment he was the equal of God, but who now acknowledges in all Christian humility that in God alone is supreme power and infinite wisdom" (p. 579).

Name _____

Attribute Web

Directions: Create an attribute web for Edmond Dantès (before he becomes the Count of Monte Cristo).

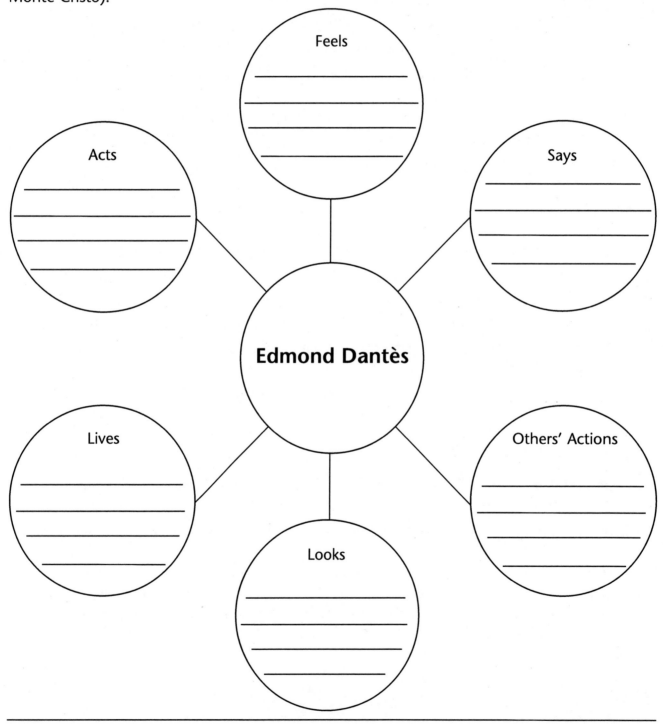

Attribute Web

Directions: Place the Count of Monte Cristo's name in the center oval. On the spokes record descriptions. On the smaller spokes beneath each spoke, give examples from the book to support the description.

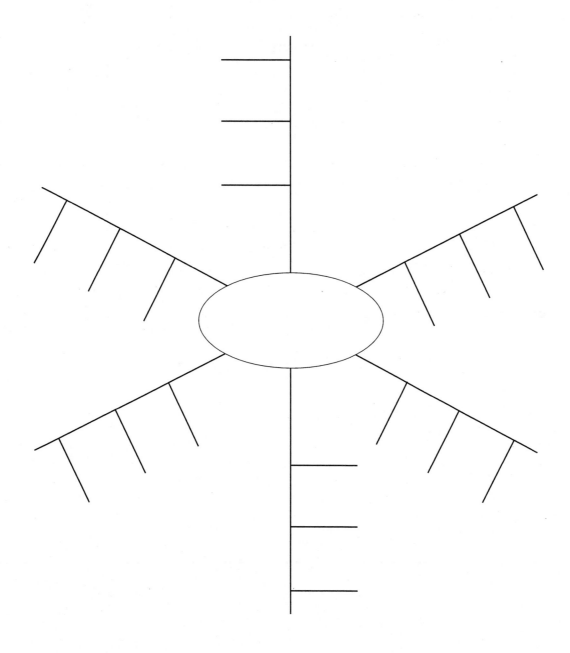

Name _____

Character Chart

Directions: In the boxes across from each of the feelings, describe an incident or time in *The Count of Monte Cristo* when each character experienced that feeling. You may use "not applicable" if you cannot find an example.

	Mercédès	Mme. Danglars	Mme. de Villefort	Valentine
Frustration				
Anger				
Fear				
Humiliation				
Relief				

Name _____

Character Analysis

Directions: List the names of Abbé Faria, Danglars, Fernand, Villefort, Noirtier, Albert Morcerf, Caderousse, and Maximilian in the boxes below. Working in a small group or with a partner, discuss the attributes of the characters. In each character's box, write several words or phrases you feel describe him.

Name _____

Story Map

Directions: Fill in each box below with information about the novel.

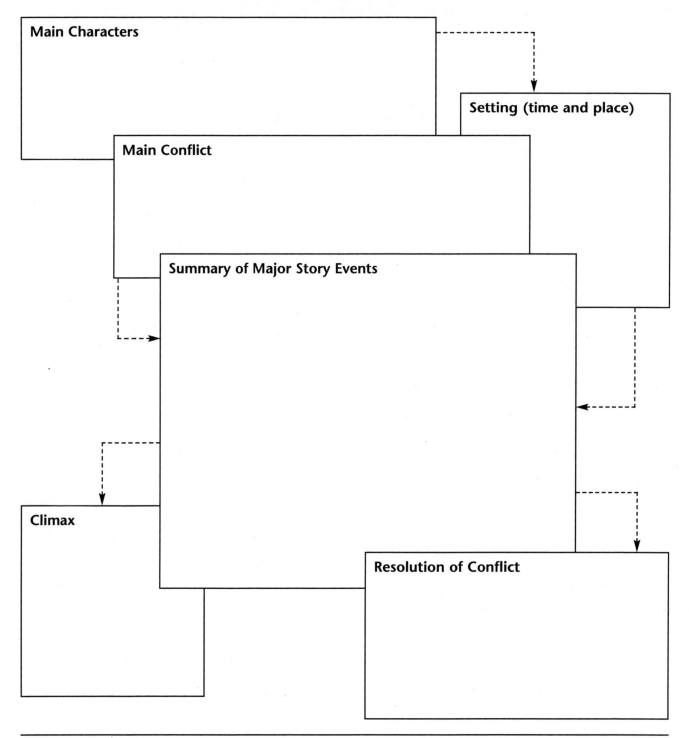

Main Characters

Setting (time and place)

Main Conflict

Summary of Major Story Events

Climax

Resolution of Conflict

Fishbone Map

Directions: List the effect (or result) in the box. Consider the causes. List cause 1, 2, 3, 4 (as appropriate). Add details to support the causes you list.

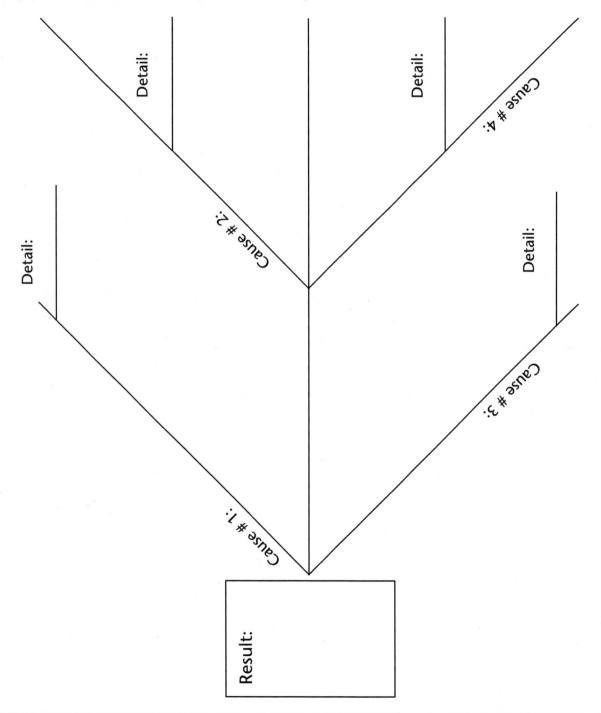

Cause/Effect Chart

Directions: When examining the reason for events in a story, we often find that

(a) one cause has several results, or

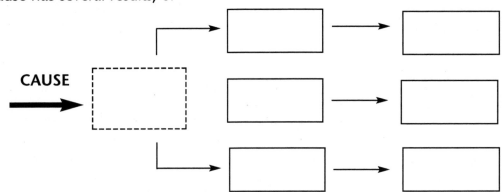

(b) several causes lead to the same result. Find an example of (a) and (b) from *The Count of Monte Cristo* and fill out a cause/effect chart for each example.

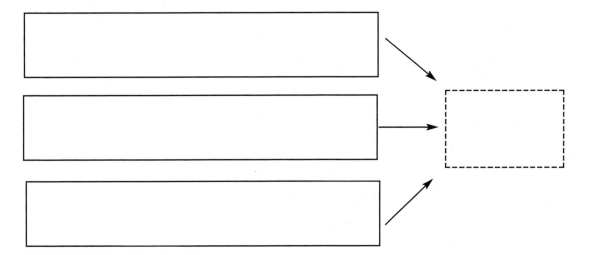

24

Name _____

Inference—Flow Chart

Directions: Fill in the boxes in the flow chart with the events portrayed in the story. In the ovals beneath, state what emotion and feeling is inferred.

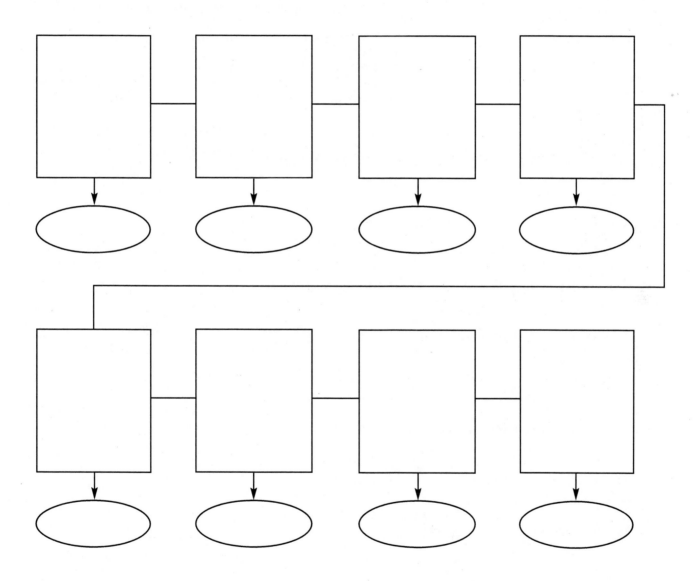

Name _____

Match each character with the correct identification.

_____   1. Edmond Dantès   a. owner of the *Pharaon*

_____   2. Danglars   b. will betray own father for political gain

_____   3. Mercédès   c. betrays another because of love for a woman

_____   4. Villefort   d. young man who is the victim of a conspiracy

_____   5. Caderousse   e. prisoner #27, Château d'If

_____   6. Fernand   f. young woman betrothed to her true love

_____   7. Abbé Faria   g. betrays another because of professional jealousy

_____   8. M. Morrel   h. manipulates an old man for money

Fill in the blanks.

9. The primary country in which the story takes place is _____.

10. The leaders of the two rival political factions are _____ and

_____.

11. The protagonist is falsely accused of being a _____.

12. Dantès learns of a treasure that is hidden on _____.

13. Dantès escapes from prison by _____.

14. Dantès spends _____ years in prison.

Match the following characters with what the Count of Monte Cristo discovers about them.

_____   1. Danglars   a. signed order for Dantès' imprisonment

_____   2. Fernand   b. kept silent about plot against Dantès; poor innkeeper

_____   3. Mercédès   c. wrote the defamatory note about Dantès; wealthy banker

_____   4. Caderousse   d. interceded for Dantès; faces bankruptcy

_____   5. Villefort   e. delivered the note about Dantès; prestigious politician

_____   6. Morrel   f. married Dantès' enemy; now a beautiful Countess

Short Answers

7. What does Dantès discover on the Isle of Monte Cristo?

8. While Dantès is in prison, what happens to his father?

9. How does the Count of Monte Cristo save the Morrel family?

10. Where does Monte Cristo first meet Mercédès' son?

11. What is Luigi Vampa's role in Albert's life?

12. What career does Fernand pursue when he leaves the army?

13. How does Mercédès initially react to Albert's friendship with Monte Cristo?

14. What does Monte Cristo ask Danglars to do?

27

True/False

_____ 1. Haydee is the daughter of the Count of Monte Cristo.

_____ 2. The Morrel children attribute the rescue of their family to one of God's angels.

_____ 3. Monte Cristo discusses toxicology with Mme. de Villefort.

_____ 4. Monte Cristo intends to invite the Morcerfs to his home in order to introduce them to the Cavalcantis.

_____ 5. Villefort's father, Noirtier, lives with his son.

_____ 6. Valentine de Villefort is happily planning her marriage to Franz d'Épinay.

_____ 7. Noirtier has the notary prepare a will that excludes Valentine in an attempt to protect her from an unwanted marriage.

_____ 8. Monte Cristo uses the telegraph to implement his plans for revenge against Danglars.

_____ 9. Danglars shows deep appreciation toward his wife for helping him amass his fortune.

_____ 10. Danglars wishes his daughter to marry Andrea de Cavalcanti.

_____ 11. Monte Cristo enjoys the food and interaction with guests at the Morcerfs' ball.

_____ 12. Valentine's maternal grandfather dies before he arrives in Paris.

Name _____

Fill in the blanks.

1. Valentine tells Maximilian she must marry Franz because _____

_____.

2. Maximilian overhears Doctor d'Avrigny tell Villefort that _____ died from poisoning.

3. Noirtier communicates "yes" and "no" answers by _____.

4. Noirtier reveals that he killed _____.

5. Haydee considers herself to be Monte Cristo's _____.

6. Haydee's father, Ali Tebelin, died tragically when she was _____ years old.

7. The doctor accuses _____ of poisoning Barrios.

8. Haydee accuses _____ of causing her father's death.

9. Albert challenges Monte Cristo to a duel because _____

_____.

10. Mercédès comes to Monte Cristo to _____.

Short Answers

1. How does Noirtier attempt to protect Valentine from the murderer?

2. What does Villefort vow to do after Valentine's "death"?

3. How does Mme. de Villefort react when she enters Valentine's room after her death?

4. How does Monte Cristo convince Maximilian not to kill himself?

5. What does Mme. de Villefort do after her "trial"?

6. In the denouement, what happens to Maximilian? to Haydee?

True/False

_____ 7. Monte Cristo assumes the alias of Abbé Faria in an attempt to save Valentine.

_____ 8. Monte Cristo's heart is softened toward Valentine when he learns of Maximilian's love for her.

_____ 9. Noirtier tells Villefort the name of the murderer.

_____ 10. Monte Cristo seals Danglars' financial ruin by reporting him to the authorities.

_____ 11. After Danglars flees, Mme. Danglars believes Debray will marry her.

_____ 12. Mercédès and Edmond's final meeting ends in anger and accusations.

A. Identification: Match each character with the correct identification. (2 pts. each)

_____	1. Edmond Dantès	a.	believes in and intercedes for Dantès
_____	2. Fernand	b.	accused of murder; becomes a victim
_____	3. Villefort	c.	betrothed to Dantès
_____	4. Morrel	d.	betrays Dantès for love of a woman
_____	5. Danglars	e.	beautiful Greek slave
_____	6. Valentine de Villefort	f.	views himself as God's instrument of vengeance
_____	7. Albert de Morcerf	g.	betrays Dantès for fear of losing political prestige
_____	8. Mercédès	h.	father figure for a hopeless young man
_____	9. Haydee	i.	imprisoned because of jealousy and greed
_____	10. Noirtier	j.	consumed with jealousy and ambition
_____	11. Abbé Faria	k.	totally devoted to his granddaughter
_____	12. The Count of Monte Cristo	l.	life is spared because of his mother

B. Multiple Choice: Choose the BEST answer. (2 pts. each)

_____ 13. Dantès is betrayed by all but which one of the following?
    (a) Fernand
    (b) Danglars
    (c) Busoni
    (d) Villefort

_____ 14. Dantès spends _____ years in prison.
    (a) ten
    (b) fourteen
    (c) twenty
    (d) five

_____ 15. While in prison, Dantès experiences renewed hope because of
  (a) Abbé Faria
  (b) Mercédès
  (c) his father
  (d) the jailer

_____ 16. Dantès' changes while in prison include all but which one of the following?
  (a) He is well educated.
  (b) His innocence has turned to cruelty.
  (c) He forgives his enemies.
  (d) He is driven by hatred.

_____ 17. The death of Dantès' father is attributed to
  (a) grief and hunger
  (b) suicide
  (c) maltreatment by Morrel
  (d) old age and anger

_____ 18. Mercédès marries Fernand because
  (a) he forces her
  (b) she feels sorry for him
  (c) of his tenderness after Dantès' imprisonment
  (d) of his promise to free Dantès

_____ 19. Caderousse reveals details surrounding and following Dantès' arrest because
  (a) the priest shows him a diamond
  (b) he feels sorry for Dantès
  (c) he hopes God will forgive him
  (d) the priest threatens him

_____ 20. The Count of Monte Cristo employs all but which one of the following aliases?
  (a) priest
  (b) law firm clerk
  (c) Signor Busoni
  (d) a ship captain

© Novel Units, Inc.

32

_____ 21. Monte Cristo aids M. Morrel by all but which one of the following?
(a) prevents his suicide
(b) gives him five hundred thousand francs
(c) redeems his bank note to M. Boville
(d) rebuilds the *Pharaon*

_____ 22. Luigi Vampa releases Albert de Morcerf in exchange for
(a) Peppino's life
(b) Franz's life
(c) one hundred thousand francs
(d) a governmental pardon

_____ 23. Mercédès' initial meeting with Monte Cristo in Paris causes her
(a) happiness
(b) terror
(c) anger
(d) to run away

_____ 24. The Cavalcantis entice Danglars because
(a) they offer him a title
(b) they are Bonapartists
(c) of their ties to the Ali Pasha
(d) of their wealth

_____ 25. Noirtier attempts to save Valentine from an unwanted marriage by
(a) threatening to disinherit Edward
(b) threatening to reveal his Bonapartist views
(c) excluding her from his will
(d) sending her to her maternal grandparents

_____ 26. Monte Cristo is able to manipulate Danglars because
(a) he knows the truth about his wife
(b) of Danglars' slothfulness
(c) he owns part of Danglars' bank
(d) of Danglars' greed and gullibility

_____ 27. Count de Morcerf's dishonor causes him to
      (a) kill his wife
      (b) flee the country
      (c) commit suicide
      (d) go insane

_____ 28. The murders Mme. de Villefort commits are prompted by
      (a) greed
      (b) grief
      (c) love for Monte Cristo
      (d) love for Valentine

_____ 29. Lucien Debray's primary motivation as Mme. Danglars' lover is
      (a) pity
      (b) money
      (c) retaliation
      (d) infatuation

_____ 30. When Danglars married his wife, she
      (a) had honor but no money
      (b) had neither honor nor money
      (c) had money but little honor
      (d) promised to make him rich

_____ 31. Monte Cristo rents a house next door to Villefort
      (a) to complete his revenge against the family
      (b) because his friend the priest needs a place to live
      (c) because he has fallen in love with Valentine
      (d) so he can watch over and protect Valentine

_____ 32. Edward de Villefort's death causes Monte Cristo to
      (a) rejoice in his vengeance
      (b) doubt his right to vengeance
      (c) leave the country
      (d) kill himself

_____ 33. Monte Cristo reveals his role as M. Morrel's benefactor
(a) to prevent Maximilian's suicide
(b) to save Julie's life
(c) because he wants the money repaid
(d) because he wants to please Mercédès

_____ 34. Mme. de Villefort's motive for killing her son is
(a) she doesn't really love him
(b) he knows the truth about Valentine
(c) she is angry at Monte Cristo
(d) she must not leave him behind

_____ 35. Valentine is escorted to the Isle of Monte Cristo by
(a) Maximilian
(b) Haydee
(c) Monte Cristo
(d) Busoni

_____ 36. Mercédès experiences _____ when she watches Albert's boat depart.
(a) anger
(b) happiness
(c) sorrow
(d) relief

_____ 37. In the denouement, Haydee symbolizes
(a) Monte Cristo's chance for a happy life
(b) the return of power to Ali Pasha
(c) the loss of love
(d) Monte Cristo's final revenge

_____ 38. The novel reveals Dantès' final act of revenge on all but which one of his enemies?
(a) Danglars
(b) Villefort
(c) Caderousse
(d) Fernand

_____ 39. The setting of the novel begins during the reign of _____.
   (a) King Louis XV
   (b) King Henry VIII
   (c) Queen Elizabeth
   (d) King Louis XVIII

_____ 40. The author of *The Count of Monte Cristo* is
   (a) H.G. Wells
   (b) Alexandre Dumas
   (c) Charles Dickens
   (d) James Fenimore Cooper

C. Essay: Choose one of the following and respond in a well-developed paragraph of at least five sentences. (10 pts.)

(a) Trace the development of the theme "vengeance" in the novel.

(b) Describe the pre-prison Dantès and explain the effects on him of fourteen years in prison.

D. Creative Response: Choose one of the following. (10 pts.)

(a) Write a diamente poem contrasting Revenge and Forgiveness.

(b) Write a letter from Monte Cristo to Mercédès five years after the end of the novel.

A. Characterization: Write two to four words that characterize each of the following. (2 pts. each)

1. Edmond Dantès
2. Abbé Faria
3. Villefort
4. Fernand
5. Noirtier
6. Mercédès
7. Haydee
8. Caderousse
9. Mme. Danglars
10. Mme. de Villefort
11. Danglars
12. Morrel (the father)
13. The Count of Monte Cristo

B. Multiple Choice: Choose the BEST answer. (2 pts. each)

_____ 14. Dantès is betrayed for all but which one of the following?
    (a) jealousy
    (b) ambition
    (c) fear
    (d) valor

_____ 15. Dantès' escape from the Château d'If symbolizes
    (a) rebirth to a noble life
    (b) rebirth to a world of deceit
    (c) death to treachery
    (d) death of all emotion

_____ 16. Dantès' changes while in prison include all but which one of the following?
    (a) He is well educated.
    (b) His innocence has turned to cruelty.
    (c) He has regressed mentally.
    (d) He is driven by hatred.

_____ 17. Mercédès marries Fernand because
   (a) he convinces her Dantès is dead
   (b) she ceases to love Dantès
   (c) he promises to free Dantès
   (d) of his tenderness after Dantès' imprisonment

_____ 18. Monte Cristo aids M. Morrel in all but which one of the following?
   (a) prevents his suicide
   (b) gives him five hundred thousand francs
   (c) redeems his bank note to M. Boville
   (d) rebuilds the *Pharaon*

_____ 19. Noirtier attempts to save Valentine from an unwanted marriage by
   (a) sending her to her maternal grandparents
   (b) excluding her from his will
   (c) threatening to reveal his Bonapartist views
   (d) threatening to disinherit Edward

_____ 20. Monte Cristo is able to manipulate Danglars because
   (a) he knows the truth about his wife
   (b) of Danglars' slothfulness
   (c) he owns part of Danglars' bank
   (d) of Danglars' greed and gullibility

_____ 21. When Danglars married his wife, she
   (a) had money but little honor
   (b) honor but no money
   (c) had neither honor nor money
   (d) promised to make him rich

_____ 22. Monte Cristo's rental of a house next door to Villefort indicates
   (a) revenge
   (b) compassion
   (c) treason
   (d) hopelessness

_____ 23. Monte Cristo reveals his role as M. Morrel's benefactor
   (a) to save Julie's life
   (b) because he wants the money repaid
   (c) to prevent Maximilian's suicide
   (d) because he wants to please Mercédès

_____ 24. In the denouement, Haydee symbolizes
   (a) hope/restoration
   (b) power/money
   (c) loss/tragedy
   (d) revenge/retaliation

_____ 25. Which of the following does NOT allude to the themes of the novel?
   (a) Supreme power and wisdom are in the hands of God alone.
   (b) Only a man who has felt ultimate despair is capable of feeling ultimate bliss.
   (c) The God of vengeance will always choose a human to punish the wicked.
   (d) God is always more powerful than man.

C. Short Answer: Write brief answers to the following. (2 pts. each)

26. What does the Abbé Faria symbolize to Dantès?

27. Identify at least three pseudonyms Edmond Dantès employs and one person with whom he interacts under that alias.

28. To what is Louis Dantès' death attributed?

29. Why does Luigi Vampa release Albert de Morcerf?

30. What is Debray's motivation in his love affair with Mme. Danglars?

31. How does Mercédès react to her first meeting with the Count of Monte Cristo in Paris?

32. What motivates Mme. de Villefort to commit two murders and attempt a third?

33. In her suicide note, how does Mme. de Villefort justify poisoning Edward?

34. What effect does Edward's death have on Monte Cristo?

35. Explain the end result of Monte Cristo's revenge against Danglars, Fernand, and Villefort.

© Novel Units, Inc.

39

D. Literary Terms: Identify the following literary devices. (2 pts. each)

36. _____ Fernand recoiled like a wayfarer at the sight of a snake.

37. _____ Death smiles on me.

38. _____ reference to Nero

39. _____ Dantès passed through the air like a wounded bird falling.

40. _____ Stars are God's lanterns.

E. Essay: Choose one of the following and respond in a well-developed paragraph of at least seven sentences. (10 pts.)

(a) Analyze and explain the symbolism of Edmond Dantès' burial at sea.

(b) Characterize Edmond Dantès—the Count of Monte Cristo. Tell what he is like at the beginning, the forces that affect change, and what he is like in the end.

F. Creative Response: Choose one of the following. (10 pts.)

(a) Write an article for a Paris newspaper speculating on the mysterious disappearance of the Count of Monte Cristo. Consider reference to the tragedies in the Villefort household.

(b) Write dialogue depicting Valentine's first meeting with her father after she "returns from the dead."

Answer Key

Activities #1 & #2: Responses will vary.

Activity #3: 1. e 2. n 3. h 4. k 5. p 6. m 7. q 8. c 9. s 10. l 11. g 12. a 13. o 14. i 15. t 16. d 17. b 18. j 19. r 20. f

Activity #4: 1. d 2. l 3. o 4. f 5. r 6. i 7. m 8. a 9. s 10. h 11. q 12. c 13. k 14. t 15. b 16. e 17. j 18. n 19. p 20. g

Activity #5: Charts will vary. Definitions: 1. sonorous: giving out or having a deep, vibrant, ringing sound 2. pseudonyms: assumed names; aliases 3. toxicology: science that deals with poisons and their effects, detection, and antidotes 4. taciturn: saying very little; inclined to silence 5. candid: saying openly what one really thinks; outspoken 6. avaricious: greedy; greatly desiring money or property 7. notary: public officer authorized to certify deeds and contracts and to attend to legal matters 8. approbation: favorable opinion; approval 9. propriety: quality or condition of being proper 10. patriarch: father or ruler of a family or tribe 11. pecuniary: of or having to do with money 12. nabob: native ruler in India; an important person 13. conjugal: of or having to do with marriage 14. presages: signs felt as warnings; omens 15. sardonic: bitterly contemptuous; coldly scornful; mocking 16. condescension: haughty or patronizing attitude 17. eccentric: out of the ordinary; peculiar; odd 18. banalities: commonplace, trite statements 19. decorum: proper behavior; good taste in conduct, speech, or dress 20. apoplectic: sudden loss or lessening of the power to feel, think, or move; stroke

Activity #6: 1. contemptuous 2. hashish 3. dispassionately 4. incessant 5. cognizant 6. austere 7. injunction 8. phenomena 9. calumnies 10. apparition 11. defamatory 12. ineffable 13. reparation 14. firman 15. compatriots 16. odious 17. flagrant 18. adherent 19. dexterity 20. cryptic

Activity #7: Charts will vary. Example—Word: implacable; Synonyms: unyielding, unappeasable, inflexible, relentless; Antonyms: tolerant, flexible, forgiving, receptive; Definition in own words: being unwilling to forgive or be reconciled to someone; Sentence: The crime committed against his family left the angry man with implacable emotions.

Study Guide

Chapters 1-4: 1. Dantès: protagonist, sailor aboard *Pharaon*, engaged to marry Mercédès; Danglars: purser on *Pharaon*, jealous of Dantès; Morrel: owner of the *Pharaon*; Caderousse: neighbor of Dantès' father who has taken most of his money as payment of Dantès' debt; Fernand: cousin of Mercédès who wants to marry her; Mercédès: Dantès' fiancée 2. died of brain fever; Dantès assumed command of the ship and has been chosen as the ship's new captain (pp. 2-3, 8) 3. Danglars: jealous and wants to be captain of the *Pharaon*; Caderousse: resents and distrusts Dantès because he has mistreated Dantès' father; Fernand: loves Mercédès and wants to marry her (pp. 11-15, 28-29) 4. He is arrested on suspicion of being a Bonapartist, based on an anonymous letter, and is taken to the deputy magistrate, Villefort (pp. 25-27, 35-37). 5. Responses will vary. 6. Activity

Chapters 5-7: 1. Villefort is the deputy magistrate who interrogates Dantès; Noirtier is his father and is a supporter of Napoleon Bonaparte. Villefort has changed his name and distances himself from his father because he doesn't want to jeopardize his own career (pp. 31, 39-41). 2. At first he is impressed by Dantès' answers and believes him; he shows Dantès the anonymous letter and concludes that jealousy is behind the plot. He changes when he realizes the letter Dantès received on the Isle of Elba is addressed to Noirtier, and he condemns Dantès to prison (pp. 35-42). 3. a prison for important political offenders; "a subterranean room whose bare and reeking walls seemed as though impregnated with tears"; "An iron hand seemed to have nailed him to the spot where he stood the night before."; "At times he would walk round and round his cell like a wild animal in a cage" (pp. 45-49). 4. Responses will vary. 5. Activity

---

Chapters 8-13: 1. to beg him to release Dantès; refuses; if she had returned and asked Villefort to reconsider in the name of Almighty God (pp. 51-52) 2. Mercédès: grief-stricken, desperate, oblivious to everything but Edmond; Fernand: takes advantage of the situation and consoles Mercédès; M. Morrel: does not give up hope and tries to gain support for him; Caderousse: restless and uneasy, drinks; Danglars: feels no remorse, is happy, believes he will become captain of the *Pharaon*, but eventually flees to Spain; Dantès' father: loses all hope and dies (pp. 52-53, 63-64) 3. Napoleon, who was exiled to the Isle of Elba after King Louis XVIII regained power, is rumored to be returning to France. Villefort tells the King he detected a conspiracy, arrested Dantès, and learned from him of Napoleon's return. Villefort proclaims loyalty to the King, maintains his position under Napoleon because of Noirtier's influence, then regains the King's trust when Napoleon is defeated (pp. 57-63). 4. In total despair, he prays first to the jailers, then to God; decides to starve himself to death; changes when he realizes another human is attempting to break through the wall between their cells (pp. 65-69) 5. Abbé Faria, an Italian scholar, has been a political prisoner since 1807, in Château d'If since 1811; intelligent and ingenious; teaches Dantès and helps him regain hope; guides Dantès to an understanding of the conspiracy involving Danglars and the others (pp. 72-84) 6. Responses will vary. 7. Activity

Chapters 14-17: 1. He knows the location of a treasure that is hidden there; shows him the paper containing the clues to the location and has Dantès memorize them; thinks he (Faria) will die soon (pp. 91-102) 2. by replacing the abbé's corpse with his own body in the burial shroud; the prison guards toss him into the sea, and he cuts himself out of the shroud and away from the cannonball weight; the skipper of a smuggler ship (pp. 109-115) 3. fourteen years; He has lost his innocence and youth and has become bitter, deceitful, and vengeful (pp. 117-119). 4. Responses will vary. 5. Activity 6. Activity

Chapters 18-22: 1. He wants the ship crew to leave him alone to explore what he believes to be the cave holding the hidden treasure (pp. 124-126). 2. uses gunpowder to blow away the rock that hides Spada's cave and finds a wooden chest bound with iron that holds untold wealth including coins, gold bars, and jewels; He falls to his knees and thanks God (pp. 129-131). 3. as a priest; knows he has a better chance to find out the truth because people trust and confide in priests (pp. 135-139) 4. tells Caderousse that Dantès confided in him before his death and asked him to find out what happened to the principal people in his life, then baits Caderousse with a large diamond; Dantès gets the following information: his father died of grief and hunger shortly after Dantès' arrest; Danglars wrote the letter that led to his arrest and Fernand mailed it; Caderousse kept silent; Morrel interceded for Dantès twenty times and now is on the brink of bankruptcy; Danglars is a millionaire banker and a Baron; Fernand fled to Spain but returned to France and is now the Count of Morcerf; Mercédès married Fernand and has a son, Albert (pp. 136-150). 5. Responses will vary. 6. Activity 7. Activity

Chapters 23-25: 1. English clerk in Rome law firm of Thomson and French: finds out about Morrel and is able to read his own prison records; buys Morrel's notes from M. de Boville; grants Morrel extension on his loan. Sinbad the Sailor: sends letter to Julie Morrel giving instructions for location of red purse holding receipt for money Morrel owes and a large diamond, thus saving the Morrel family from dishonor (pp. 150-174) 2. record of Abbé Faria's death; record of Dantès' denunciation and examination, Morrel's petition, order for Dantès' imprisonment signed by Villefort (pp. 154-155) 3. He has lost all his ships except the *Pharaon*, the shipyard is run down and only has two employees, he is on the brink of bankruptcy; uses his wealth to rescue the Morrel family (pp. 155-174) 4. Responses will vary. 5. Activity

Chapters 26-29: 1. rich, handsome, supposedly Sicilian or Maltese, gentlemanly, powerful (pp. 174, 182-183) 2. Albert de Morcerf, Franz d'Épinay; Albert is Mercédès and Fernand's son (pp. 178-179). 3. kidnapped by Luigi Vampa, a bandit; rescues him in exchange for life of Peppino, who is about to be executed; introduce him in Paris (pp. 202-217) 4. "I must own that the Count is a peculiar man,

---

and I feel very uneasy about the appointment he has made with you in Paris" (p. 217). 5. Activity 6. Activity

Chapters 30-33: 1. Lucien Debray, private secretary to Minister of the Interior; Beauchamp, a journalist; de Château-Renaud, a baron; Maximilian Morrel, now a captain in the military (p. 225) 2. He is a count and former general and commander of the Legion of Honor in the French army; he left military service after twenty years and entered politics; is wealthy and prestigious; appears careworn (pp. 236-237) 3. She watches him, pale and motionless; thanks him for saving Albert's life; probes Albert about the Count's identity and cautions him to be careful (pp. 238-242) 4. banker and a baron; reluctantly extends unlimited credit to the Count, settling on six million for the first year (pp. 245-247). 5. The Count buys them for an enormous sum; Baroness Danglars becomes irate because the horses belong to her and she has promised to lend them to Mme. de Villefort; The Count returns the horses to the Danglars, then rescues Mm. de Villefort and her son when the horses run away (pp. 249-256). 6. Activity 7. Activity

Chapters 34-37: 1. a beautiful Greek girl the Count rescued from a slave market; considers herself to be his slave although he assures her she is free; loves the Count (pp. 257-261) 2. Maximilian and Julie, who has married Emmanuel, live happily together; he sees the purse that held the bank note and diamond she received from "Sinbad the Sailor"; Julie tells him an angel from God rescued her family from ruin; Irony: The Count is the "angel" (pp. 261-266). 3. Valentine and Edward, Villefort's children, and Mme. de Villefort are there. He learns that Noirtier, Villefort's father, lives with them and is paralyzed. He and Mme. de Villefort discuss poison, especially brucine (pp. 267-276). 4. the Danglars and the Villeforts; the Morcerfs 5. Responses will vary. 6. Activity

Chapters 38-42: 1. Valentine de Villefort loves Maximilian Morrel; Eugénie Danglars is betrothed to Albert de Morcerf, son of Mercédès and Fernand (pp. 284-291). 2. Valentine: doesn't want to marry Franz because she loves Maximilian Morrel; her father: wants her to marry Franz, believing it is a good political move; Mme. de Villefort: pretends to approve but secretly doesn't want them to marry; Noirtier: opposes the marriage (pp. 292-296, 303, 307) 3. has a notary prepare a will that excludes Valentine because he thinks Franz won't marry her if she doesn't have an inheritance (pp. 297-304) 4. A telegram, reprinted in the newspaper, presents false information, leading Danglars to lose a million francs (pp. 308-309). 5. Italian nobility, a major and his son; wealthy, well-educated; son looking for a French wife (pp. 314-318) 6. Activity

Chapters 43-46: 1. They discuss money, and he tells her that each time she has given him a tip to make money, she also has enriched herself. He blames her for giving him false information that has led to current financial losses. He accuses her of giving money to Debray (pp. 320-326). 2. says he knew Morcerf when he was the poor fisherman Fernand, and his wealth has been attained during the past twenty years; The Count suggests that Danglars write his correspondent in Janina and find out what part Fernand played in the Ali Tebelin affair (pp. 330-332). 3. Mercédès invites him to walk with her to the conservatory; they talk casually; she offers him food but he refuses; he tells her he has suffered deeply, had once planned to marry but the girl didn't wait for him when he went to war; she questions him about Haydee and he tells her she is his slave. Their conversation reveals that she knows he is Dantès (pp. 343-346). 4. Valentine de Villefort's maternal grandfather; he dies (pp. 346-347). 5. Responses will vary. 6. Activity

Chapters 47-49: 1. refuses and tells him she must marry Franz in honor of her grandmother's wishes; agrees to elope when he threatens to commit suicide if she marries Franz (pp. 353-358) 2. Madame de Saint-Méran died from poison (pp. 364-365). 3. her grandfather; they love each other deeply; she needs him; he wants to protect her from marriage to Franz; reveals he (Noirtier) is the one who killed Franz's grandfather, General Quesnel (pp. 366-379) 4. terrible news connecting Fernand and Janina (p. 393) 5. Responses will vary. 6. Activity

---

Chapters 50-53: 1. Her father was the Ali Pasha of Janina. When Haydee was four years old, he was betrayed and killed by a Frenchman he trusted. The Frenchman sold her and her mother into slavery, and Monte Cristo eventually bought her (pp. 394-412). 2. alludes to slander about Morcerf and tells him the engagement is broken (pp. 415-419) 3. dies from poison; Valentine is responsible for the three deaths; refuses to drag Valentine before the courts (pp. 422-434) 4. Responses will vary. 5. Activity

Chapters 54-59: 1. He denies the charges of treason and defends himself by showing the Chamber of Peers Ali Tebelin's ring and letters of trust. The president reads a letter from an eyewitness; Haydee appears, tells her story, and identifies Fernand as her father's betrayer. He is found guilty of felony, treason, and dishonor (pp. 434-445). 2. thinks Monte Cristo is responsible for his father's ruin (pp. 445-453) 3. to beg him to spare Albert's life; Monte Cristo agrees to do so but thinks he will die instead (pp. 456-462) 4. Edmond is Death and the phantom. He will die if Albert lives, and Death and the phantom will no longer exist (p. 461). 5. Activity

Chapters 60-62: 1. She is poisoned and appears near death; daily giving her small doses of the poison to strengthen her immunity (pp. 476-487) 2. He goes to Monte Cristo and tells him that Valentine has been poisoned and is dying; Monte Cristo says it is God's judgment. Maximilian tells Monte Cristo of his love for Valentine and Monte Cristo realizes the devastation his vengeance is bringing to Maximilian, whom he loves as a son. He promises to help (pp. 482-484). 3. moves into the house next door disguised as the priest Busoni; watches over her for four nights; replaces the poison in her tumbler with a health-giving potion; helps her detect Mme. de Villefort; gives her a powerful narcotic to make her appear dead (pp. 488-499) 4. Responses will vary.

Chapters 63-66: 1. She appears to be dead (pp. 500-501). 2. The tumbler she had emptied of remaining poison is again one-fourth full (pp. 502-503). 3. claims the remainder of his credit from Danglars, five million francs, exactly the amount Danglars holds on deposit from the hospitals; Danglars flees before the hospital treasurer comes to redeem the bonds (pp. 511-517). 4. by revealing that he (Monte Cristo) is the "angel" who saved Morrel from ruin and dishonor (pp. 519-525) 5. Responses will vary. 6. Activity

Chapters 67-69: 1. They have been lovers and business partners; she thinks he will marry her since Danglars is gone, but he rejects her (pp. 528-534). 2. He has joined the military; she will live in Marseilles; buried some money in the garden of the house in Marseilles (pp. 534-541) 3. Villefort accuses her of murder and suggests that she must poison herself or he will denounce her publicly; she begs for her life; Edward, because she kills him as well as herself (pp. 546-553) 4. At first he believes the retribution is just and sufficient because of the crimes Villefort committed against Edmond. He realizes his vengeance has gone too far when he sees Edward's body (pp. 553-556). 5. Activity

Chapters 70-71: 1. They meet in the garden in Marseilles; he offers her consolation as a friend and tells her Albert is noble-hearted. He feels she is justified if she hates him, but she blames herself for being a coward and not waiting for him; he tells of his suffering in prison and how it made him wicked and treacherous. Their final "au revoir" holds the possibility of meeting again some day. 2. Maximilian and Valentine are reunited and Monte Cristo gives them his property in Paris; Haydee vows her love for Monte Cristo, and they sail away together (pp. 570-580). 3. Activity

Note: Student response to Activities #8-#15 will vary. This key offers suggestions.
Activity #8: Edmond Dantès; Acts: confident, cheerful, contented; Feels: loved, respected, hopeful; Says: he loves Mercédès, he is innocent, he must see the head of the prison; Lives: in Marseilles, France; Looks: handsome, strong; Others' Actions: Mercédès and his father—love, Danglars—jealousy and greed; Fernand—jealousy over Mercédès; Villefort—fear of losing political status.
Activity #9: the Count of Monte Cristo: deceptive (lies to his rescuers and others); manipulative (with Caderousse, Albert, Danglars, Morcerf); ingenious (his many aliases, ability to save Morrel); vindictive

44

(toward Danglars, Morcerf, Villefort); compassionate (toward Morrel family, Mercédès, Valentine, and Haydee); lonely (loses Mercédès, afraid to allow others' into his heart); bold (toward Luigi Vampa, Albert, everyone he encounters), repentant (Edward's death).

Activity #10: Mercédès: frustration—Monte Cristo refuses to eat food at her ball; anger—she realizes Fernand betrayed Edmond; fear—scheduled duel between Albert and Monte Cristo, humiliation—leaves home after learning truth about Fernand; relief—Monte Cristo agrees to spare Albert's life. Mme. Danglars: frustration—Debray refuses to marry her; anger—Danglars sells her horses; fear—that she might lose her money; humiliation—rejection by Debray; relief—horses are returned. Mme. de Villefort: frustration—poison doesn't kill Noirtier; anger—Edward is not included in Noirtier's will; fear—the tumbler in which she placed Valentine's poison is refilled; humiliation—her husband accuses her of murder; relief—thinks Valentine is dead. Valentine: frustration—loves Maximilian but betrothed to Franz; anger—everyone determined she must marry Franz; fear—realizes someone poisoned her grandparents; humiliation—not applicable; relief—awakens from "death" sleep, reunited with Maximilian.

Activity #11: Abbé Faria: kind, compassionate, intelligent, ingenious, brave. Danglars: ambitious, greedy, jealous, self-promoting, manipulative. Fernand: jealous, manipulative, cruel, liar. Villefort: royalist, concerned with self-preservation, fearful, ostentatious, ambitious, proud. Noirtier: Bonapartist, loyal, intelligent, resourceful. Albert: naïve, kind, supportive toward his mother, easily led. Caderousse: apathetic, greedy, uncaring. Maximilian: gentle, kind, proud of his heritage, loving, consumed with love for Valentine.

Activity #12: Main Characters: Edmond Dantès, Danglars, Morrel, Mercédès, Fernand, Abbé Faria, Villefort, Caderousse. Setting: Marseilles, Château d'If, Rome, Paris. Main Conflict: Dantès is betrayed and imprisoned unjustly; conflict within himself (desire for revenge) and those who betrayed him. Summary of Events: Dantès is arrested, imprisoned, escapes miraculously, returns as the Count of Monte Cristo, and begins his journey of vengeance. He saves the Morrel family from ruin, meets Albert de Morcerf and is introduced to Parisian society, manipulates and ruins Danglars financially, causes dishonor and eventual suicide of Fernand, creates situation that ultimately drives Villefort to insanity, and assists Mercédès and Albert financially. Climax: Edward dies and Dantès realizes his thirst for vengeance has driven him too far. Resolution: saves Valentine and reunites her with Maximilian, helps Albert and Mercédès financially, finds hope for happiness with Haydee. He is finally at peace with himself.

Activity #13: Result: The Count of Monte Cristo seeks revenge. Cause 1: he is falsely arrested; detail: Danglars, Fernand, and Caderousse betray him. Cause 2: he is imprisoned; detail: Villefort knows the truth but has Dantès imprisoned because he fears losing his political position. Cause 3: he talks to Caderousse and learns what happened to those from his former life; detail: experiences sorrow over death of his father and Mercédès' marriage to Fernand; Cause 4: disguised as a law firm clerk, discovers the letter Danglars wrote and the order for his imprisonment, realizes who betrayed him and how; detail: vows vengeance on all those involved and begins implementation of plan.

Activity #14: (a) Cause: Dantès' imprisonment; Results: experiences despair, meets Abbé Faria and regains hope, becomes educated, learns of hidden treasure on Isle of Monte Cristo, makes plans to escape, escapes. (b) Result: The Count of Monte Cristo realizes he cannot play God. Causes: sees the hurt and anguish in Mercédès, almost kills Albert, realizes the death of the innocent child Edward is his fault.

Activity #15: Dantès' arrest and imprisonment: fear, agony, despair. Dantès meets Abbé Faria: hope. Dantès escapes and finds the treasure: relief, joy, anticipation. Dantès saves the Morrel family: contentment, satisfaction. The Count of Monte Cristo meets Mercédès in Paris: regret. Monte Cristo ruins Danglars financially: gratification. Monte Cristo causes Fernand's dishonor: satisfaction. Monte Cristo inadvertently causes Edward's death: regret, torment, anguish. Monte Cristo sails away with Haydee: happiness, hope.

Activity #16, Quiz 1: 1. d 2. g 3. f 4. b 5. h 6. c 7. e 8. a 9. France 10. King Louis XVIII, Napoleon Bonaparte (pp. 30-31, 63) 11. Bonapartist (pp. 33, 52) 12. Isle of Monte Cristo (pp. 93-101) 13. trading places with a corpse (pp. 109-112) 14. fourteen (p. 119)

Activity #17, Quiz 2: 1. c 2. e 3. f 4. b 5. a 6. d 7. an enormous fortune of gold, coins, and jewels (pp. 130-132) 8. dies from grief and hunger (p. 138) 9. by redeeming their bank note and giving them a diamond (pp. 165-166, 172-173) 10. Rome (pp. 174-175) 11. kidnaps him and holds him for ransom (p. 204) 12. politics (pp. 237-238) 13. cautions Albert to be careful (p. 241) 14. extend him unlimited credit (pp. 245-248)

Activity #18, Quiz 3: 1. F (pp. 257-258) 2. T (pp. 263-264) 3. T (pp. 270-273) 4. F (pp. 280-283) 5. T (pp. 291-292) 6. F (p. 285) 7. T (pp. 299-303) 8. T (pp. 308-309) 9. F (pp. 320-326) 10. T (p. 330) 11. F (pp. 340-346) 12. T (pp. 346-347)

Activity #19, Quiz 4: 1. her father orders it and her grandmother wishes it (pp. 353-355) 2. Mme. de Saint-Méran (pp. 363-364) 3. blinking his eyes (pp. 368-371) 4. Franz's grandfather or General Quesnel (pp. 386-387) 5. slave (pp. 396-399) 6. four (p. 401) 7. Valentine (pp. 430-432) 8. Fernand (pp. 440-443) 9. he thinks Monte Cristo is responsible for his father's ruin (pp. 445-446) 10. beg him to spare Albert's life (pp. 456-457)

Activity #20, Quiz 5: 1. gives her small doses of poison each day to build her immunity (pp. 486-487) 2. avenge all the deaths (pp. 506-509) 3. terror-stricken, staggers to the door, disappears, faints (pp. 502-503) 4. reveals that he is the benefactor who saved Morrel's father from financial ruin and dishonor (pp. 519-525) 5. kills Edward and herself (pp. 546-553) 6. is reunited with Valentine; vows her love for Monte Cristo and sails away with him (pp. 570-580) 7. F (p. 488) 8. T (pp. 403-404) 9. T (pp. 508-509) 10. F (pp. 511-517) 11. T (pp. 528-534) 12. F (pp. 563-657)

Final Test, Level One: A. 1. i 2. d 3. g 4. a 5. j 6. b 7. l 8. c 9. e 10. k 11. h 12. f **B.** 13. c (pp. 142-143) 14. b (p. 117) 15. a (pp. 72-102) 16. c (pp. 85-103) 17. a (pp. 141-142) 18. c (pp. 147-148) 19. a (pp. 135-139) 20. d 21. b (155-174) 22. a (p. 206) 23. b (p. 241) 24. d (pp. 314-315, 329-330) 25. c (pp. 302-303) 26. d (pp. 242-246, 511-514) 27. c (p. 475) 28. a (pp. 287, 497) 29. b (pp. 532-534) 30. c (p. 531) 31. d (p. 488) 32. b (pp. 555-556) 33. a (pp. 519-523) 34. d (p. 553) 35. b (pp. 575-576) 36. c (pp. 561-562) 37. a (pp. 576-577) 38. c (pp. 475, 517, 553-556) 39. d (p. 59) 40. b (cover) **C & D.** Responses will vary.

Final Test, Level Two: A. 1. innocent victim, trustworthy, honest 2. compassionate, ingenious, intelligent, generous 3. fearful, self-promoting, politically motivated 4. jealous, cruel, subversive 5. noble-hearted, Bonapartist, intelligent 6. beautiful, innocent victim, loving 7. beautiful, loyal, appreciative, gentle 8. manipulative, apathetic, greedy 9. self-promoting, wealthy, dishonorable 10. jealous, vindictive, cruel, greedy 11. wealthy, grasping, greedy 12. honest, noble, appreciative 13. vindictive, wealthy, handsome, ingenious **B.** 14. d (pp. 142-143) 15. b (pp. 111-117) 16. c (pp. 85-103) 17. d (pp. 147-148) 18. b (pp. 155-174) 19. b (pp. 302-303) 20. d (pp. 242-246, 511-514) 21. a (p. 531) 22. b (p. 488) 23. c (pp. 519-523) 24. a (pp. 576-577) 25. c **C.** 26. rebirth, renewed hope (pp. 72-102) 27. Sinbad the Sailor: the Morrels; Count of Monte Cristo: Fernand, Danglars, Villefort, many others; Signor Busoni: Villefort; Priest: Caderousse 28. hunger and grief (pp. 141-142) 29. in exchange for Peppino's life (p. 206) 30. money (pp. 532-534) 31. with terror and apprehension (p. 241) 32. greed, wants money for Edward (pp. 287, 497) 33. a mother never leaves her son (p. 553) 34. deep agony; he realizes he has carried vengeance too far; repents (pp. 555-556) 35. Danglars: financial ruin, he flees; Fernand: dishonor, he commits suicide; Villefort: loses his wife and son, goes insane (pp. 475, 517, 553-556) **D.** 36. Simile (p. 16) 37. Personification (p. 66) 38. Allusion (p. 317) 39. Simile (p. 111) 40. Metaphor (p. 122) **E & F.** Responses will vary.

Notes

47

Notes